Working with Disney

UNIVERSITY PRESS OF MISSISSIPPI

JACKSON

Working with *Disney*

INTERVIEWS
WITH
ANIMATORS,
PRODUCERS,
AND ARTISTS

———

DON PERI

www.upress.state.ms.us

The University Press of Mississippi is a member of the
Association of American University Presses.

Copyright © 2011 by University Press of Mississippi
All rights reserved
Manufactured in the United States of America

First printing 2011

∞

Library of Congress Cataloging-in-Publication Data

Peri, Don.
Working with Disney : interviews with animators, producers,
and artists / Don Peri.
p. cm.
"In this book, as in my earlier book, Working with Walt:
Interviews with Disney Artists, you will meet Disney artists, park
cast members, and on-screen talents . . ." Introduction.
Includes index.
ISBN 978-1-60473-939-8 (cloth : alk. paper) — ISBN 978-1-60473-
940-4 (pbk. : alk. paper) — ISBN 978-1-60473-941-1 (ebook)
1. Disney, Walt, 1901–1966. 2. Animators—United States—
Interviews. I. Peri, Don. Working with Walt. II. Title.

NC1766.U52D52 2010
741.5'8092273—dc22   2010029165

British Library Cataloging-in-Publication Data available

To all the people in this book who shared their stories with me

To my family

*And to the families who lived on Chestnut Avenue in San Bruno,
California, between 1953 and 1960, especially the Silver Family
and the Wright Family, who contributed to creating a wondrous
world in which to be a kid and to nurture Disney dreams*

Contents

CONTENTS

Acknowledgments

I thank all of the people who graciously let me interview them and whose stories are in this book. I have always appreciated how lucky I have been to meet and talk with so many gifted, dedicated people.

Walter Biggins, Anne Stascavage, and the rest of the staff at the University Press of Mississippi were very supportive and encouraging as I undertook my second book for the press. Steve Yates has been very helpful in marketing my books.

Angela Parker helped me tremendously by transcribing the interviews with Sharon Baird and Bobby Burgess. Too young to have watched *The Mickey Mouse Club* in its initial run, Angela now feels like an honorary Mouseketeer.

Corky Mau assisted me by converting many of my interviews from hard copy, painstakingly typed in precomputer days, to electronic documents.

Vicki Hanson took on the thankless job of proofreading, for which I am very grateful. Of course, I am responsible for any errors that remain.

The State of California provided me with time away from work as a serendipitous result of its staff furlough program.

My wife, Sue; my daughters, Julie and Emily; and my dog, Indi (especially Indi) patiently listened to my unending stories about Walt Disney and his wonderful group of artists. I am grateful that my family has happily let me follow my passion.

Introduction*

As a child of the Baby Boom, I grew up in an America that was experiencing a wave of unprecedented prosperity in the 1950s. My early years were spent in San Bruno, California, where we lived in what I think of as a quintessential Baby Boom neighborhood. Almost all of the families had World War II–veteran fathers and stay-at-home mothers who had moved from nearby San Francisco to the new suburbs near the start of the decade. Chestnut Avenue teemed with children of all ages, so we never had to stray from our block for any kind of kid activities. Because of overcrowding in the schools, we were on a double-session schedule for a couple of years, meaning that we attended school only for half a day. We had plenty of time for sports, games, and, of course, television.

Walt Disney entered our childhood world in a big way—or perhaps I should say on several fronts. At the El Camino movie theater and occasionally at vintage theaters in San Francisco, we watched each new Disney animated feature that was released as well as the rerelease of classic features. (I remember my brother and I cried outside the theater after seeing Old Yeller [1959].) We were also enthralled by Disney's venture into live-action films. In 1954, Walt came right into our homes with his

*Portions of this introduction were taken from *Working with Walt: Interviews with Disney Artists*, (Jackson: University Press of Mississippi, 2008).

weekly television show. Within months, Davy Crockett coonskin caps sprouted all along Chestnut Avenue. The following year brought not only Disneyland, which we all dreamed of visiting and soon did, but also *The Mickey Mouse Club*. We all wanted to be Mouseketeers and faithfully wore our ears as we watched the show early each weekday evening. We even formed our own branch of the Mickey Mouse Club (of which, not surprisingly, I was president).

Walt Disney touched our lives, our imaginations, and our hearts; for some of us, that touch has never left. In this book, as in my earlier book, *Working with Walt: Interviews with Disney Artists*, you will meet Disney artists, park cast members, and on-screen talents who helped Walt achieve his dreams and ours along with him. From the world of Disney animation come top animators Frank Thomas, Ollie Johnston, and Marc Davis—three of Walt's famed Nine Old Men of Animation. They animated so many of the memorable characters in the Disney feature films, beginning with the first full-length feature film, *Snow White and the Seven Dwarfs* (1937). Dave Hand played a huge role at the studio beginning in 1930, and he was the first director (after Walt) of short-subject cartoons. He also directed *Snow White*. Lance Nolley worked at the Disney Studio as a layout artist, planning the basic composition of each animated scene. Gilles "Frenchy" de Trémaudan was a 1930's-era animator of many Disney cartoons. From across Hollywood, Walter Lantz was famous not only for his Woody Woodpecker character but also as the host of his own weekly television program, *The Woody Woodpecker Show*, which began broadcasting just a couple of years after *The Mickey Mouse Club*. He inherited Walt's first popular animated character, Oswald the Lucky Rabbit, and provided a unique perspective to that story and to the animation industry in its Golden Age as a friendly competitor of Walt Disney's. Disneyland would not have been possible without the contributions of many artists, both backstage and onstage at the park. After distinguished careers as animators, Xavier (X) Atencio and Bill Justice joined Walt's team of Imagineers at WED (for Walter Elias Disney) Enterprises, now Walt Disney Imagineering. Xavier, or X, as he is better known, has a special place in the hearts of Disney fans because he wrote the lyrics for the Pirates of the Caribbean song that inspired the attraction and the subsequent films. Bill, among other projects, directed "The Mickey Mouse Club March" on *The Mickey Mouse Club* and programmed the early audio-animatronics figures at Disneyland. Joyce Belanger, John Catone, and Van France were cast members at Disneyland on opening day in July 1955 and spent more than thirty years helping to create the magic of Walt's first theme park. Joyce worked in many areas of the park. John was the spaceman in Tomorrowland as well as a ride operator (in the Disneyland vernacular, an attractions host). Van founded the University of Disneyland and helped train cast members in the "Disney way" right from the beginning. Lou Debney, a longtime Disney employee, moved from assisting with animated and live-action films into television in its infancy and helped create the unprecedented success of Walt's ventures into this new medium. One of the most exciting and innovative efforts in children's programming, *The Mickey Mouse Club* starred Sharon Baird and Bobby Burgess, along with Annette Funicello and the other Mouseketeers who left an indelible mark on those of us fortunate enough to watch the show in its initial run. The Walt Disney Company has subsequently honored seven of these interviewees with the Disney Legends Award.

My lifelong interest in Walt Disney blossomed into an avocation in 1974 when I met Ben Sharpsteen (featured in *Working with Walt: Interviews with Disney Artists*), a retired Disney animator, director, and producer. Together, we wrote his memoirs about his thirty years at the Disney Studio, most of which he deposited in the Walt Disney Archives, where scholars have utilized it. Drawing on that experience and extensive independent research, I began teaching courses on Disney in particular and animation in general; more significantly, I continued my research over the next seven years by interviewing a group of key artists from the Walt Disney Studio. Meeting Ben Sharpsteen—someone who knew Walt Disney—inspired me to seek out as many of the early Disney artists as I could find. Even as early as 1974, death had robbed the world of an alarming number of Disney artists, starting with Walt Disney himself in 1966. So each time I traveled from my home in northern California to southern California, I tried to interview as many people as I could squeeze into my schedule. Fortunately, I had an opportunity to talk with all of those I sought, sometimes just shortly before they passed away.

In 1985, I interviewed a group of Disneyland cast members, including Joyce and John, over the phone from an office building in San Francisco. As I sat in an urban canyon, looking out at skyscrapers, in the background at the other end of the call I could hear the whistle of the Mark Twain Riverboat plying the Rivers of America. Between 2002 and 2007, I conducted another series of interviews, this time for the Walt Disney Family Foundation. Thus, the interviews in this book took place between 1976 and 2005. I have been very privileged to have had the opportunity to meet and hear the stories of so many of Walt's people, including the fifteen who appear in this book.

I have concentrated on the people who created the Disney magic—on the big screen, on the little screen, or in the parks—and their relationships with each other and especially with Walt Disney. My interviews offer a fresh perspective on Disney, not only because of the range of people with whom I talked but also because of the subjects we discussed. I had the opportunity to interview many of them when they were still relatively young with sharp minds and vivid memories. Unfortunately many are gone now, but they will live on as they share their stories through the pages of this book.

Some of the interviews were conducted at the studio, some by mail, some by phone, and some at the interviewees' homes. At the studio especially, an interesting phenomenon would often take place during an interview when interviewees often would gradually slip from the past tense to the present tense when referring to Walt—not "Walt did this" or "Walt did that," but "Walt does this" or "Walt does that." (In the text, I have kept references to Walt Disney in the past tense.) In spirit, Walt was still there, and at times I almost felt like I would soon hear his signature cough as he came down the hall, about to rush into the room with some fantastic new idea.

If I ever needed a reason to pursue the people who knew and worked with Walt Disney, artist Herb Ryman (also featured in *Working with Walt: Interviews with Disney Artists*) summed it up very nicely when he said to me, "So each person that you talk to and each person you interview will have a little part of the puzzle, the jigsaw puzzle, that goes into the portrait of Walt Disney. It is for people like yourself to have the privilege and the duty of presenting Walt as a human being and a person who can be known, a person who you can be close to."

As I gathered the information and taped the interviews—analog recordings in the beginning, digital later on—I wanted and needed to learn as much as I could about this magical man. And a serendipitous result of all this was that I had an opportunity to meet and to know so many wonderful people—many unknown to most of the public then— who helped make the difference at Disney. The people you will meet in the book are not unbiased (if anyone ever could be). They admired, respected, even loved Walt Disney, but all of them experienced the full force of Walt's personality. I have conducted more than ninety interviews to date, and the word interviewees most often used to describe their feelings about Walt is *awe*. They were then and for the rest of their lives in awe of him.

When I conducted my early interviews, only a few books and magazines dealt with animation (the best of which was Mike Barrier's *Funnyworld*). In those days before the Internet, it was not easy to know who else was working in this field. I have often felt that we early historians were a little like medieval monks working on our own in our cells. Only later, when I started meeting other historians conducting similar research, did I realize the excitement of talking with kindred spirits, people who spoke my language. Now we have so much access to information that it is at times overwhelming, but back then, it was a much smaller world.

Each trip to southern California was a wonderful foray into the world of Walt Disney, as the people I met would reveal facets of Walt's personality and his style. I was discovering that each person had his or her own Walt Disney. No two people saw him in the same way. No matter how big or little a person's role, Walt touched his or her life, and the stories about him add to the mosaic of Walt himself. With each interview, I learned more about Walt, but I also came to understand that to have a complete understanding of the man would be an elusive dream. Yet I wanted to continue to pursue this dream. But that did not mean I should give up my dream. I "knew" Walt Disney as the avuncular host of his weekly TV show and thought of him as a warm and genial man who seemed to have an endless supply of curiosity. For years, I only had that image of Walt and the Walt of the studio publicity department. But they were more than enough to keep my interest in him alive. After I began interviewing more and more people, my fascination with him grew by leaps and bounds.

Walt Disney was born in Chicago on December 5, 1901. He moved with his family to Marceline, Missouri, in 1906, where he spent the golden years of his childhood living in a rural and small-town setting. In 1911, the family moved to Kansas City, Missouri. Walt had many jobs as he moved from childhood to adolescence, most notably as a newspaper boy and a "news butcher" (vendor) on passenger trains. After serving with the Red Cross in France as World War I came to a close, Walt worked briefly as a graphic artist for Pesmen-Rubin, where he met another graphic artist and future animator, Ub Iwerks, whose career became forever linked with Walt's. Walt then moved on to the Kansas City Film Ad Company, where he became fascinated with animation. He formed Laugh-o-Grams Pictures and produced a few films before bankruptcy closed down the fledging studio.

At the time Walt Disney entered the world of animation, the art form had grown by leaps and bounds from the fledgling work of J. Stuart Blackton (*Humorous Phases of Funny Faces* [1906]) in America and Emile Cohl in France (*Fantasmagorie* [1908]) to Winsor McCay's triumph, *Gertie the Dinosaur*, which appeared as part of an interactive performance with McCay (1914). New York became the center of the animation business, and many early innovations, such as the use of clear plastic celluloid sheets (cels) so that animated drawings could be overlaid on opaque background drawings, were becoming standard industry practices. The output of Pat Sullivan, with his immensely popular Felix the Cat, Paul Terry and his Aesop's Fables, Max Fleischer and his Out of the Inkwell series, and a host of other studios producing animation fare for theater bills dwarfed tiny Laugh-o-Grams. Walt was influenced by the work of these men; for his Alice Comedies, he chose to reverse the novelty used in the Out of the Inkwell series. Walt recalled, "They had the clown [Koko the Klown] out of the inkwell who played with live people. So I reversed it. I took the live person and put him into the cartoon field.

I said, 'That's a new twist.' And I sold it. I surprised myself." Despite
their prolific output of short-subject cartoons, the New York studios
were not seriously regarded by most of the filmmakers or the distribu-
tors. For the most part, these cartoons served as fillers on theater programs, although some characters—most notably, Felix the Cat—became
quite popular.

With a working print of *Alice's Wonderland*, Walt headed for Hollywood. In 1923, he and his brother, Roy O. Disney, formed the Disney
Brothers Studio, which was renamed Walt Disney Productions in 1926.
Between 1924 and 1927, the studio produced fifty-six Alice comedies,
all of which combined live action and animation until their popularity
waned. The Disney brothers then produced the animated series Oswald
the Lucky Rabbit. Both series garnered some success, but they were not
the best cartoon series of their day. That would change soon. In 1928,
Walt lost his access to the Oswald character and most of his studio staff
to the series' distributor, Charlie Mintz. With only Iwerks and a small
staff remaining, Walt launched his next cartoon creation, Mickey Mouse,
who debuted with his girlfriend, Minnie, in *Steamboat Willie* (released on
November 18, 1928), and the rest, as they say, is history. The film—third in
the series but the first with sound and the first released as talkies swept
the nation (sound was later added to the first two films)—was an enormous hit and began what would become the Golden Age of Animation
at the Disney Studio. But at the time, Walt was in desperate need of staff
to meet his production goals, so in addition to hiring raw local talent, he
recruited animators with experience from the New York studios. In 1929,
Walt launched a second series, the Silly Symphonies, with *The Skeleton
Dance*. Iwerks, who animated almost that entire cartoon, left the studio
to go into business for himself in 1930 but returned to the studio ten
years later and remained there for the rest of his career, making enormous contributions in the development of animation technology.

With the success of the Mickey Mouse cartoons, Walt constantly
pushed for better draftsmanship in the animated drawings, taking
advantage of each innovation that came along, beginning with sound
and then color (*Flowers and Trees* [1932]) and later the multiplane
camera, which added three-dimensional depth. He stressed story

development and personality development at a level that was unique at the time. *Three Little Pigs* (1933) is the first film to succeed in creating characters with individual personalities. He wanted audiences to believe that his characters were real, and the success of the short subjects proved that he was on the right track. His success at branding the Disney characters was so great that the old *Life* magazine ran a cartoon in which a dejected would-be movie patron turns away from the box office, saying, "What? No Mickey Mouse?" In just a few years, Walt had almost single-handedly raised the quality of cartoons from a novelty to an art form. Other cartoon producers— Fleischer, Terry, Harman-Ising, Van Beuren—produced cartoons that in some cases rivaled Disney in artistic style (Harman-Ising) and had characters with popular followings (Fleischer's Betty Boop, for example), but Walt's mantra of "plussing"—constantly striving to improve every aspect of the cartoon medium—kept him at the forefront with audiences and critics as well as with his competitors. As Chuck Jones of Warner Bros. said, "Of course we stole from Disney then. *Everybody* stole from Disney then." Walt received a special Academy Award for the creation of Mickey Mouse and dominated the short-subject category throughout the 1930s: *Flowers and Trees* (1931–32), *Three Little Pigs* (1932–33), *The Tortoise and the Hare* (1934), *Three Little Orphans* (1935), *The Country Cousin* (1936), *The Old Mill* (1937), *Ferdinand the Bull* (1938), and *The Ugly Duckling* (1939).

In 1925, Walt married Lillian Bounds, and they became parents to daughters Diane in 1933 and Sharon in 1936. Even though short-subject cartoons were immensely popular, Walt could not recover his costs because of the high quality he demanded for each cartoon output. As a huge leap forward in the development of animation, Walt launched his studio into feature-film production with the highly successful *Snow White and the Seven Dwarfs* (1937). The film was so profitable that Walt and Roy could afford to move from their studio on Hyperion Avenue to a new studio they designed in Burbank. With the success of *Snow White*, Walt embarked on several features, including *Pinocchio* (1940), *Fantasia* (1940), *The Reluctant Dragon* (1941), *Dumbo* (1941), and *Bambi* (1942). As would be the case throughout his career, wherever Walt directed his attention and energy, the studio shined, and that is where Walt's staff wanted to be. Few other studios attempted animated feature films at that time, with the exception of a couple of rather weak productions emanating from the Max Fleischer Studio.

By 1939, World War II had begun in Europe, cutting off the highly lucrative foreign market; as a result, only *Dumbo* was a success on its initial release. The studio strike of 1941 was a very bitter experience for many of those who struck as well as for those who did not, and that bitterness persisted for many years. The studio had grown so quickly over the preceding dozen years that it had lost its intimacy, and some of the dissatisfaction was an inevitable result of that growth. But with Hollywood studios battling the union movement, some of the factors that led to unrest at the Disney Studio included a bonus system that had become dysfunctional as the staff grew very large with feature productions, a suspension of raises as the studio experienced financial challenges, a fear of layoffs, and a clash between staff who wanted to unionize and Walt and Roy, who had run the studio in a paternalistic manner when the staff was smaller and more manageable. (Many staff members liked the way Walt and Roy had run the studio.) The strike was ultimately settled through arbitration, but tension and anger remained. Among those who did not strike, sympathies ranged from strong support for the management position and hostility toward the strikers to an understanding of the point of view of those on the bottom rungs of the corporate ladder, who were paid the least and had little job security.

The attack on Pearl Harbor and the U.S. entry into World War II brought the Disney Studio contracts for training films and public-service films, which became a mainstay of production through the war years. A few feature films were made: *Saludos Amigos* (1943), *Victory through Air Power* (1943), and *The Three Caballeros* (1945). In the first years after the war, with the exception of *Song of the South* (1946) and *So Dear to My Heart* (1948), which were combination live-action and animated films, Walt turned to feature films comprised of animated shorts: *Make Mine Music* (1946), *Fun and Fancy Free* (1947), *Melody Time* (1948), and *The Adventures of Ichabod and Mr. Toad* (1949).

During the 1930s and 1940s, other studios focused on short-subject cartoons, moving away from the Disney style of realism and personality animation and pushing in different directions. Disney alumni Hugh Harman and Rudy Ising started animation studios within Warner Bros. and MGM that were in many ways the most successful rivals to the Disney style, offering a wackier, more brash and irreverent style that became very popular. Bugs Bunny, Elmer Fudd, Daffy Duck, and Tom and Jerry could hold their own with Mickey, Donald, Goofy, and Pluto. Many Disney animators enjoyed these films as members of the audience but felt that their studio was striving for something different. As Disney interest in short subjects waned with the ascendancy of feature films, Academy Awards for short subjects reflected this shift and the emergence of MGM and Warner Bros. as rivals in this field: *The Milky Way* (MGM, 1940), *Lend a Paw* (Disney, 1941), *Der Fuehrer's Face* (Disney, 1942), *The Yankee Doodle Mouse* (MGM, 1943), *Mouse Trouble* (MGM, 1944), *Quiet Please!* (MGM, 1945), *The Cat Concerto* (MGM, 1946), *Tweetie Pie* (Warner Bros., 1947), *The Little Orphan* (MGM, 1948), and *For Scent-Imental Reasons* (Warner Bros., 1949). The 1950s would be the last decade dominated by mainstream studio cartoons: double features and other changes in theatrical programming all but eliminated the market.

The 1950s saw a major resurgence of activity at the Disney Studio. Animated features returned in full force with *Cinderella* (1950), *Alice in Wonderland* (1951), *Peter Pan* (1953), *Lady and the Tramp* (1955), and *Sleeping Beauty* (1959). Walt also produced live-action films, starting with *Treasure Island* (1950) and a host of films shot in Great Britain as well as *Twenty Thousand Leagues under the Sea* (1954), *The Shaggy Dog* (1959), *Third Man on the Mountain* (1959), and many more. He also moved into the nature and documentary field with the True-Life Adventures and the People and Places series. What Baby Boomer could forget Walt's entrance into the television arena with *Disneyland*, *The Mickey Mouse Club*, and *Zorro*? And, of course, Disneyland opened right in the middle of the decade on July 17, 1955.

The 1960s carried right on with more animated and live-action features, culminating in *Mary Poppins* (1964), Disney exhibits at the New York World's Fair, and early work on what would become Walt Disney

World in Florida. Much to the sorrow of his family and friends, his staff, and all those whose lives he touched, Walt Disney passed away on December 15, 1966.

Walt Disney was a major figure of the twentieth century and a powerful force in the world of popular culture. But the stories in this book are also about the man. Walt rose from modest beginnings to the top of his field, making his story a manifestation of the American Dream. In many ways, he personifies a Horatio Alger hero, exemplifying the "ABCs of success" (Ability, Breaks, and Courage). Walt was a shrewd judge of his own ability and that of others and pushed himself and them to unimagined heights. He benefited from some breaks, like the profusion of artists available and eager to work during the Great Depression, but he also made his own breaks. He was constantly striving for something better, from sound to color to personality animation to increased realism in his cartoons, to feature-length animated films, to live-action films, to television, to theme parks, to trying to solve the plight of our cities. His were "Walt-made" breaks. He had the courage of his convictions. He took on new challenges and made animation into an art form. He persevered when the pundits were assailing him with choruses of Disney's Folly, because he believed in himself and he succeeded. And Walt liked people. That trait may appear unremarkable, but many of his decisions, both in the early days of his studio with his staff and later at Disneyland, were driven by his philosophy of giving people more than they expected. He cared about people, and they responded and reciprocated.

In 1997, I was so fortunate to meet Diane Disney Miller, Walt's daughter. Our ensuing friendship and professional collaboration led to my involvement with the Walt Disney Family Foundation and its production of a CD biography of Walt Disney, *Walt Disney: An Intimate History of the Man and His Magic*, that was introduced at a special event at Disneyland. In June 2000, the foundation invited me to participate in a documentary, *Walt: The Man behind the Myth*. And in October 2009, the foundation opened the Walt Disney Family Museum in San Francisco. The museum is spectacular and worthy of such a figure as Walt Disney. Walking through the museum—only twenty-five miles from where I grew up and first discovered the Disney magic—and seeing photos of so many people I had met over the years and again hearing their voices, I felt truly grateful to all of them for allowing me to come closer to a world within my world where the wonder and excitement of childhood still lives.

Explanation of Terms

SWEATBOX was used as both a noun and a verb by Disney veterans. Originally, the sweatbox was a tiny room about the size of a closet. The closet became a makeshift projection room in the early 1930s at the Hyperion studio site. Animators would sweat because of the closeness of the room and/or because of the anxiety of having their work analyzed and scrutinized. Even after the move to the Burbank studio and spacious projection rooms, the term *sweatbox* was still used. *Sweatbox* became a verb when someone would sweatbox a work in progress or analyze it to see if it was ready to move on to the next stage of production.

INBETWEENERS animate the fine gradations of movement in between the extremes made by an animator.

BREAKDOWN is an intermediate drawing between the animator's key drawings.

LAYOUT ARTISTS create the set in pencil where the animation action will occur.

BACKGROUND ARTISTS paint the opaque scenes that appear behind the animated cels and are involved with the color styling of the scene.

CLEAN UP ARTISTS refine the animator's rough drawings into a finished drawing that will appear in the film.

INKERS AND PAINTERS transfer the cleanup drawings to transparent celluloid. Inkers trace the drawings on the front of the celluloid or cels, and the painters fill in the color on the reverse side.

THE TRAFFIC DEPARTMENT included entry-level staffers at the Disney Studios who literally moved materials from one department to another. Many Disney artists began in the Traffic Department and praised their tenure there as a great way for them to learn about all the facets of animation production and get a sense of where they might best fit in.

WED [WALTER ELIAS DISNEY] ENTERPRISES was the design and development company founded by Walt Disney in December 1952. It was initially involved with the design of Disneyland. Walt sold WED to Walt Disney Productions (later the Walt Disney Company) in 1965. WED moved from the Burbank studio site to Glendale, California, in 1961 and is now known as Walt Disney Imagineering.

UPA (UNITED PRODUCTIONS OF AMERICA) was an American studio started in the 1940s that pioneered significant new directions in animation styling, content, and technique. *Gerald McBoingBoing*, an Academy Award–winning short subject (1950), brought UPA to the attention of the animation world. UPA is also well remembered for its Mr. Magoo cartoons. Amid Amidi's *Cartoon Modern* is an excellent resource for more information about UPA.

Note about the Interviews

I believe that history is interactive, and while I have tried to ensure the accuracy of names and dates referenced in the interviews, the stories are more challenging. How someone remembers an event may be as significant as what really happened. Readers who are curious need to do some follow-up on their own—in a sense, verifying if what they have been told in the interview is correct. Does the story match what they have previously heard or read? Is this a new facet to a familiar story, or does the account demonstrate the effects of time on memory? Is the version presented in the interview wishful thinking, or could it be the rounding of edges as stories move along through the years? Readers should remember that everyone likes to present themselves in the best possible light.

Working with Disney

Frank Thomas

Frank Thomas was born on September 5, 1913, in Fresno, California. Interested in art at an early age, he attended Fresno State College and Stanford University, where he met Ollie Johnston, who would become a lifelong friend and a fellow animator. Frank subsequently studied at Chouinard Art Institute in Los Angeles. On September 24, 1934, Frank joined the Walt Disney Studio as employee 224, thereby beginning what would be one of the most celebrated careers in animation. After working on short subjects, Frank joined the team on Disney's first feature-length film, *Snow White and the Seven Dwarfs*, where his animation of the dwarfs grieving at Snow White's bier was a breakthrough that brought audiences to tears. Over his forty-five-year career, Frank set a standard of sincerity in animation that few others could meet and none could surpass. He was a key figure on almost every Disney animation feature produced during that period, including *Pinocchio, Bambi, The Adventures of Ichabod and Mr. Toad, Cinderella, Alice in Wonderland, Peter Pan, Lady and the Tramp, Sleeping Beauty, 101 Dalmatians* (1961), *The Sword in the Stone* (1963), *Mary Poppins, The Jungle Book* (1967), *The Rescuers* (1977), and *The Fox and the Hound* (1981). One of Walt Disney's Nine Old Men of Animation, Frank's influence on the industry is immeasurable. When he and Ollie retired, they continued to provide guidance to animation through the books they authored: *Disney Animation: The Illusion of Life*, *Too Funny for Words*, *Walt Disney's Bambi: The Story and the Film*, and *The Disney Villain*. Frank was inducted as a Disney Legend in 1989 and passed away on September 8, 2004. He and Ollie Johnston profoundly influenced subsequent generations of animators, and Brad Bird has given them cameo animated appearances in two of his films, Warner Bros.' *The Iron Giant* and Pixar's *The Incredibles*.

I interviewed Frank at the Walt Disney Studios on March 26, 1976. He was only my fourth interview so I was still on a steep learning curve. But he was generous in allotting me time during his working day. According to my notes about my visit,

Frank Thomas was standing out in front of the Animation Building [after the guard had called him upon my arrival] and met me there. We went in and walked down a hall adorned with an aerial photo of the studio, early photographs of Walt and his staff, some beautiful backgrounds and set-ups from *Cinderella* and all of the major releases, and a lot of cels from this new movie they are working on, *The Rescuers*. [In Frank's office,] there was a big drawing board with a drawing on it that looked like a knee joint or maybe a knot on a tree, drawn in blue pencil. I really couldn't tell because it hadn't been finished. Part of a human skull was on top of a stack of papers. There were some drawings of a gorilla. Silver model heads of the three fairies from *Sleeping Beauty* sat on top of a cabinet behind his drawing board. There was also a movieola right behind the chair where I sat. It was bigger and more complicated than I had imagined.

This first interview led to warm friendship with Frank over the years, in which we kept in touch by mail and occasionally in person, usually through the wonderful hospitality of Howard Green, who would arrange dinners with Frank and Ollie and their wives and with Joe Grant. I treasure Frank's letters that were filled with news, enthusiasm, self-deprecating humor, advice, and an occasional irresistible barb that was so typical of him. Our Christmas card usually has a photo of my family in front of our 1938 Standard Oil Santa Claus. One year, we did something different, and I heard about it from Frank right away. So every year for the rest of his life, we made sure the Santa was featured on our card and we have kept it there ever since in Frank's memory. I feel honored to have known Frank for almost thirty years.

DP: What was your first impression of Walt Disney?
FT: I think I was probably more impressed with his product than I was with him as a person. I didn't have very much contact with him. You know, I'd see him around the halls, and he seemed to be a nice enough guy. He'd say "Hi," and I'd say "Hi." But there wasn't anything until I got further along. I was working for Freddy Moore. He had a lot of footage on a picture with the little pigs [*Three Little Wolves* (1936)]. It was more than one guy would normally turn out. I was responsible for about two hundred feet or something like that. Walt called me in because he thought it ought to be divided to get the picture out: "You've more than you can handle." I said, "Gee, I don't [think so]," because I wanted to do it myself. I thought I was the only guy who could do it, naturally, because Freddy had told me how he wanted it. Actually, I wasn't that good, but I didn't realize it then. So that was probably the first time I talked to Walt. He gave me a long piercing look and said, "Well, okay, if you think you can do it, we'll let you try." So all my first meetings with him were very favorable that way. He seemed to have a good impression. He seemed to like what I was doing and believed in what I was saying, which is more than I did. So I didn't get into any kind of pressure situations with him. It was all just a good pleasant relationship for a long time.

DP: I guess when you came to Disney, he was already well established. Did he seem to fit the image that you had in your mind, or did he seem more down-to-earth than you might have thought?

FT: Maybe I was awfully naive, but I didn't really think that much about people and what they were like. You see, I'd come down here to go to art school. First of all, I wanted to be an industrial designer. Then I was talked into switching over to magazine illustration. Cartoon[ing] had always been fun for me, but I never thought of it as a lifework. Here's a chance to do that. I just wasn't sure that I wanted to stay with this business, yet every day it got more interesting, more intriguing to me. The further I went in it, the more I was hooked on the thing. So Walt was just another guy who was making a success of what he was doing. I don't know, maybe I thought of him like a teacher I had at college or something of that sort. He was young, and he wasn't a boss behind a desk and didn't smoke cigars or a pipe [although he was a heavy cigarette smoker]. There was nothing about the image. He was just a guy who worked with you. I would hear stories about things he had done to someone or how mad he'd got. He didn't always get mad; he had other ways of dealing with it! The guys would try to put things over on him or get by with something.

What kind of personality? Boy, it was years later before I really began to be aware of that. Since he's gone and looking back on the things he did now that we have the problems that he had, we begin to say, "God, how did he do it? How did he handle it? How did he keep twelve hundred people all working on a product and know which each one was on? How could his mind conceive of this? His personnel work—how could he pick out what was the right way to go with something?"

DP: How did he sleep at night with all these problems?
FT: Yeah! At the time, none of that impressed me at all. I probably was cocky enough to figure I could do it, too, if I wanted to.

DP: In some of the articles I've read, some people say the shorts are the best that Disney did, and after that, the pictures were becoming too realistic. Other people single out *Pinocchio* as the best. Some people I've talked to think that no zenith has been reached and that maybe the next film will be the best. Do you see a peak in the art?

FT: No, that oversimplifies it too much. The way I size it up, at the time Walt started, the potential of animation—no one realized what was there really. He just figured, "Here's something that I can use." He was always looking for what can you do with it, [thinking,] "What can I make of this thing?" He never took a thing as it was and sold it. There was always his curiosity about what can you do. So he got interested in animation, [thinking,] "What can we do with this?" getting new ideas and stimulating thought. To me, he reached his peak really of what I like to do in animation with *Snow White*, because it was the richest in personality development and yet the simplest and strongest in story concept. Its popularity over the years makes me feel that I'm right in feeling that this was a peak. Now, that is not to say that it in any way reached a peak in the whole art of animation, because Walt never wanted to do the same thing twice. He was always going on to something else. So we went on to *Pinocchio*. It was the most elaborate picture, but it was quite weak story-wise. But as far as elaborate stuff to look at—pretty stuff on the screen— it was just a knockout. It cost too much money to do any more of that, so we simplified it, and we went to *Fantasia* and *Bambi* and *Dumbo*. If there had not been the war, which is what ruined *Fantasia*, and if *Fantasia* had gone over better, we've often wondered where would we be today, because Walt was reaching out and reaching out and reaching out. Because of the war, he had to turn around and come back in. He could no longer expand. But the possibilities—oh, it's just unlimited! Guys have said, "Whatever you can dream of, you can do in animation." From that point on, [after] *Fantasia*, there's been very little searching, really. He did it with a lot of those package pictures—*Make Mine Music, Melody Time*, things of that sort—where he could take little shots which were different and which might have been Silly Symphonies in the old days and experimented with them to see what he could do with them. But he was always reaching out, always searching—a terrifically creative mind.

Well, now, if you could have gone on with the staff he had—twelve hundred well-trained men, very creative men—he could play them against each other, he could shock them, and he could do all sorts of things, who knows where we would have gone. So I don't feel that you ever reached a zenith. I feel that you were expanding like this, and because of economics, you had to turn back in on yourself. When he did *Cinderella*, he had to be sure it was a safe picture because his market was still uncertain. Well, it was solid—the returns on *Cinderella*—so now he was back in business, but he couldn't experiment as wildly as he had before. So he went on to *Peter Pan* and began doing these other pictures, like *Alice in Wonderland*. So by then, he had used up the ideas that he had always had about cartoons, and by the time he got to *Sleeping Beauty*, he said, "Well, I've never had a chance to think this one through," which meant to me this was the end of the line. He'd also thought of [the stories] "Beauty and the Beast" and "Reynard the Fox." He'd thought of a half a dozen things, but he'd never got hold of them. Now, all these other pictures in his own mind he'd got hold of. He knew kind of what he wanted to do with them. But by the time he got to *Sleeping Beauty*, that was the end. Well, at the same time, he was finding out that there was a great interest in all these other things: the TV show, the park, the live-action pictures, *The Mickey Mouse Club*. So while some of us wanted to go the way we'd been going after *Fantasia*, he didn't have the interest to go that way. He'd say, "Oh, oh, I don't know." He was harder to sell on a new idea. He'd say, "Why don't you do this? It's a good product." And so we made good pictures. One thing that he kept asking for was refinement, refinement, refinement, until somebody joked that the last picture we would make would be *The Life of Christ*. And someone said, "Yeah, on the head of a pin!" It was no longer the broad cartoon. Well, that's another way to go, the perfection of illustration. If you go to any of these animation festivals and see the work that's being done around the world, all the different mediums that are explored, all the different ways of doing things— drawing direct on film, all sorts of combination things, double exposures, tricks under the camera—ways of saving money, ways of getting different effects. My golly! When I think of the different things I've seen over forty years of showings and festivals, lots of them, I don't know how they did it. So much is being done and experimented with, and no one knows. There's never been a central agency to collect it all. Each person did it his own way. Now, the things we did in *Fantasia*, the art has been lost.

We see broken, rusted equipment out here in back. "What was that?" Someone says, "Oh, I think they used that as a tub to wash something or other. They had some kind of acid in there." "What'd you use it for?" "Oh, I don't know. I can't remember." We see results on the film. We say, "Now, this is what we want to do in this sequence here." A guy says, "Well, the fellows who did that are all gone. I don't know how you do it." So it's hard. You lose the technique unless you're going to be using it.

So to get back to your original question, what was the zenith? When did you make your best picture? I think the pictures we made were almost all the best possible for what we tried to do and the conditions under which we did them. Now, to compare them, which was the best picture, I don't think you can do that.

DP: The depression certainly made people more available.

FT: It made artists available. If there hadn't been the depression, Walt wouldn't have had all these artists to draw from. But today, you try to get artists, and you get a different breed. Very talented fellows, but they've got different drives and different disciplines. The fellows with the talent that Walt had partly came out of a different type of training—what they could make themselves do, what they would do to achieve a goal—which the kids today don't have. They're looking for a different type of result.

DP: I was interested in what you thought of some of the work that other studios were doing in the 1930s, 1940s, and 1950s. Was there a competitive feeling, or did people here enjoy these cartoons but figure, "It's just not ours, but it's okay for what it is"?

FT: Individually, we laughed as hard as anybody at the work those guys did. I loved Bugs Bunny and Daffy Duck. I thought some of the things were kind of childish, but some of the things that we were doing were kind of childish—again in the matter of taste, personal opinion, judgment in these areas. For instance, there was a gag in the *Three Little Pigs*, the wolf goes down the chimney and sits in the pot of boiling water that has turpentine in it. Well, that gag must have been used twelve times by other studios, and each one trying to top it. Norm Ferguson had done the scene where [the wolf] was running along dragging his fanny on the ground. The other guys carried it further than that and had him hit rocks and go over sharp things and try to get more out of the gag. It just gets over the hill in the matter of taste and judgment and wasn't any funnier. It just became more specialized.

During the war, I was down in San Antonio, Texas, and saw a Tex Avery cartoon in a big theater. The place was just packed on a Sunday afternoon. I can't remember what the feature was, but this came on and I thought, "Oh, boy! This is going to kill 'em. This is really going to kill 'em. I love Tex Avery." And the house was absolutely quiet the whole ten minutes, because it was too sophisticated for them. And I realized— and I'd heard [it] before, but it had never really dawned on me as such before—how easy it is to be specialized, to be a professional. You laugh at things within the industry and forget that the poor audience out there, it's way over their heads. They don't know what you're talking about.

So, what do you think of the other pictures? That gets back to I like *Snow White* the best and I told you why. I love to work on funny stuff, and I thought we made some awfully funny pictures, and I thought that on the outside they made some funny pictures. But my own taste went— as you say, we were going in a different way—well, we weren't entirely because some of our Donald Ducks were as funny as anything that Tex Avery or Chuck Jones did.

DP: I was wondering if there was a rivalry, a competitive feeling that "It's our product, so it's better because it's ours."
FT: At that time, you didn't have very much exchange between the studios. We had siphoned off some of the better men around there, and maybe there was a little indignation about that, from their standpoint. I don't know that we looked down on them so much; we just didn't know who they were. They were shooting for a different type of picture than we were, generally speaking. When they got something funnier than we had, we laughed our heads off at it. I do think there was a feeling from their standpoint that Disney, they are the big snobs up on top of the hill.

DP: But probably everybody does that with the one that's on top.
FT: Yeah. Once the union came in and the cutback here at the studio, particularly after the war, then there was a lot more moving from studio

to studio. And the way things are set up, you don't lose your insurance and your sick pay and your benefits. You can go from studio to studio without losing any of those now. So now everyone in the industry knows everybody else. You see a piece of work and you would say, "Hey, that looks like so-and-so's," and you find out it was.

DP: I gather from some of the articles I've read that there were certain perimeters within which a more realistic approach was used here and that other studios would sometimes focus more on impossible gags: going from one spot to another faster than possible.

FT: Most of those speed gags came from *The Tortoise and the Hare*, and once again, we were the first to do it. Ham Luske is the one who did it, and he did it because of a test that Frank Oreb, an assistant to one of the animators, did. He did a test and he just had the character—a fish, as I recall—just practically disappear, he went so fast. Ham was quick to appreciate the value of that, so when he did *The Tortoise and the Hare*, he had the hare go that fast, and then he got the credit for having established it. So zip gags are still going on today. It's the cheapest way to cover the ground.

We look on those things partly as a swipe of someone else's idea but mainly as a cheaper way of obtaining a result. And if a guy will stoop to taking somebody else's stuff and do it cheaper, well, then, naturally you don't think as much of him as you would if he added something to somebody else's idea.

DP: I am interested in the studio strike because I understand from talking to people that not only were feelings strong at the time but that it was a real crisis. I have read accounts that portray Walt Disney as a tyrant because of the way he treated people and other accounts that say he was just a victim of a lot of things that were happening. I was wondering what was your reaction to it?

FT: At the time, I was very emotionally involved, as all of us were. When we first moved into this building, we had our coffee shop; we had our switchboard girl at the end of each wing who was supposed to know where we were. Anything you wanted, you just picked up the phone and said, "Hazel, get me a milkshake." "Hazel, get me the Buick place."

"Hazel, get my car greased." "Hazel, buy a dress for my wife." Anything you wanted, you just picked up the phone and went on working, because that's what Walt wanted. He wanted the best for his guys. Well, that's real paternalism. To me, I thought, "This is terrific." To someone else who reads it as paternalism, [he might think,] "He's not going to tell me what to do." It's hard for me to understand, but I know an awful lot of people felt that way. If you combine that with the fact that because of the war coming on, he had to cut his staff in half, he had to lay off six hundred people, [the worry about] which of the six hundred it is going to be makes for a terrific amount of unrest. Because we had ballooned up to so many people, there were inequalities in salaries. We were trying to work that out, and Walt was trying to set up boards at the various levels with the guys he could trust to work out the salary things, guys who knew who did what work. So all of this was real good thinking on Walt's part, but at the same time, he was the boss, and he wanted to be paternalistic, and he wanted to run things his own way. So, naturally, as the representatives from the union pushed him, he fought back instead of bending with it and saying, "Okay, you guys do this, and how about working out some kind of a deal?" which would have been the easy way to do it. At the same time, I think it's been pretty well proven that [there] was communist leadership of the whole union thing and the membership did not realize it themselves. They were being taken. They were being controlled. They were being duped. But the guys that Walt saw were the leaders. They came up and pounded on his desk. The guys in the union membership wouldn't do that. Walt said, "There are a lot of guys in this business who are no good at it. If I found out I wasn't right for a business, why, I'd go do something else." A guy said, "Like what?" He said, "Well, I don't know. I'd open a hamburger stand or something," which to us made perfect sense, because many of us felt that way: "Well, I'm certainly not going to spend my life in a business I'm no good at. I'd do anything else and get out of it." But an awful lot of people felt, "I've put in ten years in this business, it has to take care of me. I've got a car, I've got a wife, I've got a house, I'm not going to give up."

DP: From what I've read and heard about the strike and what led up to it, it seems like one of the hardest things is applying job security to something like talent that is so intangible. Like you were saying, if somebody does a better job than somebody else, they might have received a bonus or more money. How do you equate the two?

FT: That's particularly difficult. Terribly difficult. So many egos. In my experience, a man's creative ability is in direct relation to his ego, and some of them handled it better than others. Many guys had more talent than they could handle, and it was just driving them and driving them, and they couldn't find a balance and they took to drink or to whatever. When you get a whole bunch of those guys—now, they were for the most part rugged individuals who had no use for a union—and you balance them against what we call the hack artist, the commercial artist, the guy who's been making his little drawings day after day—you need a certain amount of those[, too]. They're looking for security. They know they're never going to make it big. They're going to hang onto anything.

DP: If you could have changed Walt Disney, would you have changed him, or how would you have changed him?

FT: I wouldn't tamper with him! No, there were many things which made me awfully mad, and many things which made me awfully upset, and he had a way of getting you so fired up and then letting you down, and sometimes he would do it on purpose and sometimes he'd do it just because his interest was in other areas. If you were mature enough and well enough balanced within yourself, you could laugh it off and absorb it. But if you're caught up in the whole thing and really got yourself in it, that's what he was able to do, to make each person contribute themselves. You were doing work above your head. You were thrilled with what you were doing. There was an excitement about it that you can't generate by yourself. He'd generate it in you. You'd get so high, it was awful tough to keep your balance, and when you'd be dropped, why, it was a shattering experience. He'd shelve the picture you were working on. He'd take you off an assignment and put someone else on it. That's what I mean by being dropped.

DP: What was it like to work at the Disney Studios in the 1930s? I realize that this is a really broad question, but was that the kind of feeling—just getting really excited about what you were doing?

FT: Yeah, and the fact that we were discovering things which had never been known before. Someone would run down the hall and say, "Hey, did you see the test Dick Lundy got?" "No, no, no! What's he got?" "Oh, wait 'til you see it!" Everybody would go running into Dick's room. Fifty guys would come in during the day to see his test. Word got around the studio. "How'd you do it?" "How'd you time it?" "Let's see the drawings." Bill Roberts had a good one. Somebody else had a good one. There was all this excitement about what you were doing. The pictures you were making had never been made before. So everything about it. When you think of the good old days—it's funny, it's those six years, from 1934–35 to 1940–41—just that little pucker there that stands out above everything in the thirty years that followed.

DP: The Golden Age that they refer to.

FT: Yeah. Now, when you talk about the best pictures and when the zenith was reached and things like that, this might have an influence on that: the fact that during those years there was the excitement of discovery, while after that, there was the perfection of technique. But there is still some discovery going on even in the perfection of technique. But the big raw idea [was done]. I keep thinking of guys like Einstein— nineteen, wasn't he, when he had his big idea? He spent the rest of his life refining it. That's kind of the way Walt went, too. As creative people, we—the two or three that I talk with—resented being forced to refine. We wanted to stay with the big ideas, keep going. And as I mentioned before, had *Fantasia* gone over, I think we would have found ourselves in another field. But Walt kept hunting himself. I don't mean to say that he curtailed his creative efforts. For instance, he loved Hiawatha.

DP: The short subject?

FT: No, just the idea of Hiawatha. He'd done that just as a short. No, but as an idea, the poem. He said, "Unlock your thinking. Try to think of something new. There is something in that that people like. There's a magic to it. There's mystery to it. There's something in that subject matter." He said, "I don't know what it is. Don't think film. Maybe it's live. Maybe it's in a theater out in the woods. Maybe it's on a mountaintop. I don't know where the thing is or what you do with it, but there's an idea there that someone could get hold of." Well, this is the way he was all the time. "An idea there that somebody could get hold of." No limitations on him.

DP: Do you think that moving to Burbank took away some of that feeling or that excitement? Was it exciting to move here?
FT: It was necessary! We were practically standing on top of one another.

DP: I understand you had about six locations. People were all over.
FT: Yeah, all over. It was like Parkinson said in his laws: the amount of output is in direct relationship to the number of phones in the building. If there's one phone and sixty people, you get a whale of a lot of stuff out. But when you have sixty phones and one person, no work ever comes out! However, while we were sitting on top of each other, we turned out a lot more exciting things than when we all had our own comfortable little rooms. And yet *Bambi* was made over here. *Fantasia* was made half over there and half over here, so I don't think the mood here really affected the product.

DP: Probably everything that happened at the time, the war—
FT: I would say the two biggest things were the war and the social unrest that came with it, which brought about the union.

DP: You had mentioned that Walt liked to put together people who didn't necessarily love each other's work.
FT: Who were opposed. Basically, if you have two people who agree with each other, all they're going to put up is what they agree on. If you have two people who disagree, who say, "You're crazy, it shouldn't be that, it ought to be this," then Walt felt that rather than sit in a corner and sulk, they were going to try to prove that their way was right and they were going to work harder to try to find a way to sell it. They were going

to try to get it past this other guy to Walt, or they were going to try to convince the other guy. They were going to work and work and work. So that was his theory, and it was 50 percent right. But no more than 50 percent! I think he wasted an awful lot of energy through that, but he also got some fantastic results. Well, he had his own way. Someone was saying the other day that he had his own way of reacting to each person individually, so if you have three hundred people, you have three hundred different Walts, because they all saw a different side of him.

Ollie Johnston

Ollie Johnston was born on October 31, 1912, in Palo Alto, California. He attended Stanford University, where his father was a professor of romance languages and where he met Frank Thomas. Just shy of graduation, Ollie came to Los Angeles to take classes at the Chouinard Art Institute. He followed Frank and other Stanford alumni to the Walt Disney Studios, joining the staff on January 21, 1935. After learning the ropes of animation on short subjects, Ollie received his big break as an assistant to Freddy Moore on *Snow White and the Seven Dwarfs*. Ollie would treasure his time with Freddy for the rest of his life and subsequently kept Freddy's pencil taped to a window as a constant reminder of the magic that flowed from it. Over the years, Ollie, as one of Walt's famed Nine Old Men of Animation, went on to work on a total of twenty-four features, including *Pinocchio, Fantasia, Bambi, Song of the South, Cinderella, Peter Pan, Alice in Wonderland, Lady and the Tramp, Sleeping Beauty, 101 Dalmatians, The Jungle Book, Robin Hood* (1973), *The Aristocats* (1970), and *The Rescuers*. After he retired, he and Frank Thomas produced four books—*Disney Animation: The Illusion of Life, Too Funny for Words, Walt Disney's Bambi: The Story and the Film*, and *The Disney Villain*—that guided generations of animators and

artists. Ollie retired in 1978 after forty-three years with the studio and was named a Disney Legend in 1989. The last survivor
among the Nine Old Men of Animation, he died on April 14,
2008. The celebration of life for Ollie at the El Capitan Theater
in Hollywood that August was also a farewell to an era of giants
who made animation the defining art form of the twentieth
century.

I first met Ollie when he sent me two tape cassettes to
record Ben Sharpsteen's answers to questions he and Frank had
posed as part of their research for *Disney Animation: The Illusion of Life*. When I brought Ben's answers to the studio, I had
lunch with Frank and Ollie, dressed in matching blue cardigan
sweaters. I interviewed Ollie at the Walt Disney Studios on
September 1, 1977. Over the years, I enjoyed exchanging letters
with Ollie and treasured every opportunity I had to visit him.
On one memorable visit, he brought out his electric train and
we were his passengers on a ride around his Flintridge backyard.
Then he let me take the controls and pilot the train around with
my daughters as passengers, and then he even gave the controls
to my oldest daughter, who was probably about eight years old
at the time, and I was her passenger! On one of my last visits,
Ollie, then age ninety, explained how Pinocchio looked back at
the Blue Fairy through his legs—and demonstrated the pose.
He was a wonderful friend, a great artist, and he left an indelible mark on all who knew him and his amazing animation.

DP: The last time I was talking with you and Frank, I hadn't known that
you had an interest in trains. Was your interest prior to Walt's interest
that led to his *Lilly Belle* train?
OJ: I had always been interested in locomotives, particularly steam
locomotives, so in about 1946, I started building this backyard railroad.
One Christmas, oh, maybe a year later, why, Ward Kimball came into
the room and he said, "Hey, I hear Walt's got a Lionel [train] set up
in a room off of his office up there for his nephew, Roy [Roy Edward

Disney]. Let's go up and see it." So we went up and walked in. Pretty soon, Walt came in. Walt said, "Gee, I didn't know you were interested in trains." I said, "Yeah, I'm building a backyard railroad." He says, "Jeez, I always wanted one of those." He'd always been interested in trains. He'd been out and ridden on Kimball's big one [narrow-gauge steam engine]. So anyway, he came out to where we were building mine in Santa Monica two or three times and watched the progress. Finally, he called in a guy from our [train] club who designed an old-fashioned locomotive that turned out to be the one that he eventually had running around his place. And so we used to exchange visits: he'd come up and ride mine, and I'd go out and ride his. So in a way, I kind of say, I stimulated his interest, which was already there. I wouldn't want to claim credit, because he used to ride the trains all the time when he was a kid.

DP: Did you find him to be a different person when you were doing that than at the studio? Was he always essentially the same type of person?
OJ: No, he was more relaxed. I would say you were kind of in awe of this guy all the time, even outside of the studio or wherever you met him, so it was a little difficult to get on the same basis with him that you would with some other worker here or some other animator. So I found I wasn't uneasy around him, but here was this famous guy, he's your boss, and you respect him a lot, and somehow I never could quite think of him as a friend! I guess I had too much respect for him, but he did relax a lot more, and we talked a little about work. He'd talk a little about a lot of the financial problems coming out of the war. Of course, there were the banks and stockholders and all kinds of things to deal with he'd never had before, and occasionally he'd comment on something about that, like, "Jeez, I hope I can get this place so it doesn't hang on a single picture one of these days," which he did shortly after that [when he] brought out the nature stuff [True-Life Adventures].

DP: Yeah and then Disneyland.
OJ: Yeah, those things added up, too. And he used to talk a little bit about trying to finance the park. He'd talk about putting his railroad around

his new house and whether his wife was particularly enamored with the idea. But he was interesting to be with at any time.

DP: I would assume that a lot of your fellow workers would envy you for having something special like that in common with him.

OJ: I remember one guy who was head of the animation department at that time kidded me and said, "Don't dance too close to the queen!" Walt used to keep coming down to my room to show me every time he'd get a new part made or something, and that sometimes was a little touchy, but nobody really kidded me much about it. I didn't think there was any jealousy, because in the first place just because I had the same hobby with Walt didn't mean that I had any strength with him that I wouldn't have had otherwise, as far as my ability in animation. I think everybody knew that. There was no way you could butter Walt up. I would never have tried. I mean, it was obvious that you couldn't, and anyway, who would want to get ahead that way with a guy like that?

DP: Going way back, I was wondering how you happened to go to work here?

OJ: When I was attending Stanford, why, they didn't have any life classes [in the art department]. Mrs. Stanford, way back in the early 1900s, had come in and found a nude model there, and she said no more models. So we had to drive up to San Mateo two nights a week to work from a model in a little small private art school. That was okay, except it was rather difficult to do. But we got credit for it in school. But anyway, Frank graduated and came down here. I came down as the manager of the football team to a [University of Southern California] game and visited him and saw the work he was doing. [I thought,] "Oh, my gosh! Look what I'm missing!" Just nothing up there comparable to this. So finally at the end of the quarter, I decided that that's what I wanted to do, and so I made arrangements to get credit at Chouinard's and that I intended to go back. All I needed was a little over a year to go back and graduate. I would spend a year at Chouinard's and then take a quarter back at Stanford and graduate. Well, while I was at Chouinard's, Jim Algar, a guy from Stanford, came down, and that was six months after

I'd come down here, and he got a job at Disney's in July of 1934. Then they were looking for people. And another Stanford fellow, Thor Putnam, went out there in early September, and then Frank went out later in September. They were all taken on. I kept getting the word back from them that they wanted more people and that I'd have a good chance, and so finally in January, I took my samples out and they said, "Okay, you can have a tryout." So I tried out for a week, drawing three little pigs—a guy with a flute, another with a drum, and [another with] a flag. You had to do a drawing, an inbetween, in a half hour. By the end of the week, I was doing that, so I was hired. January 21, 1935.

DP: Do you remember your first meeting with Walt Disney?
OJ: The first story meeting I was ever in with him—I'd passed him in the hall, you know, and he'd always said hello, but I didn't know whether he knew who I was or anything—I became Freddy Moore's assistant, so I was called in to a big story meeting on *Snow White and the Seven Dwarfs*—how the dwarfs were going to walk and all that stuff. Everybody was acting out different walks and looking pretty ridiculous. Yeah, I remember that meeting. It was over on the soundstage, and Walt was telling us about the picture and asking for ideas.

DP: As you got into animation, was it hard to have to act out something?
OJ: They filmed some of it, but they found it wasn't too successful. The animators generally are what you'd call inverted actors. I mean, they have the ability to visualize, and they observe acting and all that, but most of them aren't what you'd call real good actors themselves. And if they are, they don't animate, they act. But Walt was a good actor. He did very well. As Fred's assistant, why, I was in on all the sweatboxes on *Snow White*, with Walt and Fred and Dave Hand. That was a real privilege.

DP: I would think it would have been a real break to be his assistant.
OJ: Oh, it was great.

DP: I am impressed with how highly respected Fred is among animators. He's in a different class.

OJ: A certain aura about Fred Moore. He was such a nice guy. Actually not a complex guy, but he had this ability to draw with so much appeal, and he also had so much facility in his drawing. His drawings were so pleasingly handled as far as the line went. But Walt really rode him during *Snow White*, trying to get the best out of him. Boy, those sweatboxes, every week practically, why, he'd pick on every little thing. Fred would get kind of upset, but it brought out the best in him.

DP: The particular period that I find fascinating is the 1930s. What was it like to work here then?

OJ: Well, that was awfully nice. The place was small, and if you were in the right spot, you had quite a bit of contact with Walt. He was so enthusiastic at that time—very critical, but he believed in what he was doing. Gee, I have the feeling that if the war hadn't come and the strike, why, we would have discovered a lot more things, because that was in a period of experimentation, and he was trying all kinds of things to get the right effect—I mean, every facet of the business. It wasn't just in animation, but it was in the effects and the music and the color and the story ideas.

DP: It just seems like this burgeoning thing.

OJ: Yeah, everything was blossoming up through *Fantasia*. I mean, there's a fantastic piece of stuff, and all the new ideas that we tried in there. You just can't believe it. Well, we've never gone back to that, because it wasn't financially possible. But if the war hadn't cut off the funds, it's possible that Walt would have tried and experimented more. I don't know how much longer he would have stayed interested to that extent, but he was certainly interested at that period.

DP: I understand that after the experimenting, there was the refining of technique. Were you and the other animators aware that things had changed, or was the change kind of a gradual thing?

OJ: Oh, no, you knew. It was just like chopping something off, because when the war came and we finished up *Bambi*, then that was it. We started to do a little on *Wind in the Willows* [part of *The Adventures of*

Ichabod and Mr. Toad], but it was obvious you couldn't go ahead with that. We went on to the training films and everything, and then there was an awful lot of apprehension about whether Walt was even going to keep the place. We used to hear these rumors from stockbrokers that Walt was going to sell. And it wasn't until I got to working on the locomotive with him that I heard enough directly from him that I knew he wasn't going to do that. But you could tell the approach, for instance, on *Cinderella*, the first complete [animated] feature after the war. Why, that was laid out practically in live action, as you may know. Walt said, "Let's have a script and stick to it." And so that's what we did. That limits you in a lot of ways because [even if] you find a character that's coming off real well, you can only use him where he is in the script.

DP: I would imagine that would have taken something away from the work. And like you were saying, you don't know how long Walt would have kept up his interest in animation. *Sleeping Beauty* is the film that's often mentioned where Walt was off doing other things, such as developing Disneyland. Did that create a certain insecure feeling for you animators?

OJ: Well, it was frustrating because you couldn't get anything okayed until he had time to look at it and go over it, so I think that was one reason we spent more money on that picture, because we were on one thing too long. It was very hard to pry anything away from him. As he used to say to me when he was working out in the shop, "I've got to have a project, a new project." And he was all wrapped up in the Disneyland project and the TV shows. So his interest was so divided—when he'd come into a meeting, he would be interested and all that, but he didn't give it the thought after the meeting that he usually would have. He didn't live that stuff anymore.

DP: I have read of a story meeting that was held during the early production of *Snow White* at which Walt supposedly acted out the entire story. In one account, it said that it was so memorable that two years later people could remember how he did it. Do you recall anything like that?

OJ: Well, I'm sure he did that for people around here that were higher up than I was at the time—and probably did it for a lot of his friends on the outside! I know when he accepted the special Academy Award for *Snow White*, why, he told the whole story of *Pinocchio*. I'm afraid he might have bored the audience, because he went on at great length.

DP: That's interesting, because all I know about is the footage of Shirley Temple presenting the award.

OJ: He'd get so excited about this stuff. He wasn't quite that way on *Bambi*. I think he had a stronger feeling about *Dumbo* than he did *Bambi*. He actually left it pretty much up to us. He'd come in on meetings, and he offered a lot of helpful suggestions, but he wasn't in on it the way he was with *Pinocchio* and *Snow White*. I didn't work on *Dumbo*, but for some reason, I look at that picture and I can feel more of Walt in that than I do in *Bambi*. All that keen pathos that he got in there.

DP: Did *Bambi* draw criticism for its perceived antihunting message?

OJ: Yeah. *Field and Stream* or maybe another similar magazine or maybe more than one complained about it. Actually, on *The Rescuers*, in the window of the Pawn Shop was an old NRA (National Recovery Act) sign. Somebody from the National Rifle Association thought that we were taking a poke at them and said he'd never see another Disney film.

DP: I have a question about the strike. On my last visit, you were talking about certain practices that went on before the strike that were discontinued after—something having to do with a coffee shop.

OJ: There used to be a coffee shop right out here, down the main hall, and that was really nice, because you could get a milkshake any time of day, or coffee, or a sandwich. Of course, there were a lot more artists here then. There are more people here now, I guess, but then they were all artists. And we really appreciated it. You could call Traffic and they would deliver you a milkshake at three in the afternoon or whatever you wanted. But the same people were always sitting out there, and Walt saw them sitting there, so he finally closed it. The same thing happened to the commissary. We had a counter set up over there that was open at 7:15 in the morning or something like that. You could come out here and get your breakfast. Then it was open most of the day, I would say, until maybe 4:00 in the afternoon. But when they closed this place, they all went over there. Just couldn't stand success.

DP: That would be nice, having that kind of—
OJ: Oh, yeah, it was great! You used to be able to eat up in the Penthouse Club most of the afternoons. You can still eat lunch up there, but you used to be able to go up in the morning and get a snack and go up in the afternoon and get a milkshake or something. But that's now just open for lunch.

DP: Was the Penthouse Club just for the Animation Building or was it open to others?
OJ: The Penthouse probably caused some problems. They had to draw the line somewhere, because there wasn't room for everybody, so you had to be making a hundred dollars a week to join the Penthouse, and that really bugged some people. How else could you have decided it? I don't really know. I suppose you could have put a high membership fee or something of about five hundred dollars, which would have done the same thing. Or, I don't know, it would be pretty hard to say only the top animators or something. So what they did was to do it by the amount of money you made, and I'm afraid that was one of the points in the strike that a lot of people believed in.

DP: It amazes me because it was so long ago, but with almost everybody I've talked to, the strike seems to be still an emotional issue—emotional in the sense that everybody has vivid recollections of things involved with it.
OJ: I could never forget it. I came through a picket line for ten weeks, and as I recall, the studio was closed down for three weeks while an arbitrator come out from Washington. It was scary to us, and I didn't like going through the line. There were a lot of my friends out there. A lot of them I used to see in the evening—you know, we'd get together. But it ruined a lot of families. There were a lot of divorces. Some guys never got financially back on their feet again. It was really a tragic thing. I'd say there were a lot of reasons for it.

DP: There seem to have been a number of practices that went on earlier—the incentive system and some of those things—that in retrospect
look like they would have naturally caused some problems when they
probably weren't intended that way at all.

OJ: Not in the least. Walt really tried to take care of everybody. There was
just too much of an influx of talent all at once. The guys weren't patient
enough to wait until he sorted things out, and I guess they didn't feel
that one guy could make those decisions. I don't know, really. And then,
of course, there were certain people who just felt there ought to be a
union, period, because there was a union at MGM and Warner Bros.
and the other studios, so they wanted a union here. They went about it
all the wrong way and got tied up with [the Brotherhood of] Painters,
Decorators, and Paperhangers [of America], which was a communist
outfit. The only meeting I went to, where [Herb] Sorrell talked, he said,
"By gosh, we're going to take care of our people. We're going to see that
you have nice toilets." Here we just moved into this beautiful new building! He was talking to a different type of person.

DP: Of all these different films that you've worked on over the years, do
you have particular ones that are your favorite films? Is there one of all of
them that you feel the best about?

OJ: I loved working with Fred on *Snow White*. I didn't get to do much
animation, because Walt asked me to wait until the end of the picture
and do the assistant work for Fred. I guess I have a real soft spot in my
heart for *Pinocchio*, because that was the first feature I animated on,
really. Gee, I lived every minute of it. I believed everything in it, and I
felt like I was living in this world where Pinocchio lived. But actually,
I've had a lot more interesting characters to work with than Pinocchio.

DP: Did you work on the character of Pinocchio?

OJ: Yes.

DP: I noticed that in Leonard Maltin's *The Disney Films*, he lists you as a
character designer for that particular film.

OJ: Frank and I started on the thing together and designed the character. We were using a speeded-up voice. Walt, I guess, or the story

guys picked the voice of Ted Sears. But Walt didn't like the voice, so he junked that, and we went on to a short [subject] and then came back on it again later. At that time, he decided to use a kid's voice [Dickie Jones]—more appeal. I think at first he was thinking of a puppet that wasn't any particular age. Maybe he would have a different voice when the puppet came to life. There were all types of things that I enjoyed in *Pinocchio*—the fantasy particularly. There were tender moments in it, like with the Blue Fairy and her relationship with the cricket, which I thought was great. Then there was the more grim type of fantasy, where these boys were sold on Pleasure Island and what happened to them when they started turning into donkeys, which I thought was a real exciting way to use the fantasy. I mean, where else can you do that but in an animated cartoon? And to get inside the belly of a whale. The whole thing—gee, I thought it was beautifully conceived. A lot of people call it the finest picture we've made. There was an awful lot of money spent on it. You look at Pinocchio's costume and all the little detail down the side of the pants—gee, you can't believe all that stuff. But there are characters that I enjoyed working on more.

DP: Do you have one character that you liked the best?
OJ: Gee, I always liked what I was working on. But looking back, I enjoyed doing Mr. Smee [in *Peter Pan*]. I enjoyed doing the dogs on *101 Dalmatians*. I enjoyed working on Bambi and Thumper. I enjoyed being part of *Fantasia*, though there wasn't any what you'd really call personality-type animation, which is what I really like.

DP: Did you work on "The Pastoral?"
OJ: Yeah. I guess I loved working on Baloo and Mowgli in *The Jungle Book*. I loved working on the geese and Uncle Waldo in *The Aristocats*. And I loved Prince John and Sir Hiss [in *Robin Hood*]. I guess that was probably the richest character relationship I ever had. I enjoyed the albatross and the cat and the mice and the girl [in *The Rescuers*]. The girl not as much, but I still enjoyed it, because I felt we were doing something on that picture that would draw the audience into it and you had to have the girl to do that. The mice—you couldn't make them sympathetic, although I think they were entertaining.

DP: When you have a voice like Terry Thomas for Sir Hiss and Peter Ustinov for Prince John, do you naturally gear the character towards that voice when it's a recognizable voice?

OJ: You're influenced greatly. A lot of people said that the longer I drew Prince John, the more he began to look like Ustinov.

DP: Did you watch movies of him?

OJ: No. I watched him when he came over here and recorded. I watched him at lunch. I watched Terry Thomas, but you don't really approach it too much that way. We got certain little gestures out of Bob Newhart [for Bernard]. He's always moving his hands around when he's fumbling through a word, but mostly you use the voice. If the voice is a good one, it will make you see pictures in your mind of how this thing ought to be acted. It really doesn't have all that much to do with how that guy acts when he's performing in a role himself. He gives you a mental picture of how that ought to be acted, and more important almost than that is he gives you a personality along with story conception that his voice fits into. But you, of course, alter your story conception to a certain degree when you get a voice that deviates a little. You go with it. You don't fight it. We built a little different relationship than had originally been planned. Originally, Sir Hiss was to be a little more like Kaa in *The Jungle Book*, a little more of a villain. But it seemed more entertaining if he was submissive to Prince John. His whole existence depended on how he could butter the guy up.

DP: Has the Xerox system altered the way you animate?

OJ: It's more altered the way we clean up the animator's drawing, the way the assistant does.

DP: Does it detract or make any difference as far as the finished product?

OJ: Well, some people have complained because they thought it didn't have the refinement that the ink line has. However, I think it has more vitality, because it's the actual drawing—it isn't a tracing of the drawing, so it's got more life. With the development of different colors, we're arriving at ways to use it where we can get almost the same thing we had with the ink [line].

DP: In *The Rescuers*, the scene where the albatross is trying to fly and drops off the edge of the roof really amazes me.

OJ: We had a really tricky pan there. When he goes off the roof, first you see him disappearing from you. But then you have a scene where he's pulling out of the dive. I don't know how much you know about our pan backgrounds, but when you're diving, you've got to have a pan that's going the opposite way from your dive. Well, then, if you shift in that same scene to a horizontal move, then you've got to switch it to a horizontal pan instead of a vertical pan. That was tricky, but we worked it out and gave a good effect, because it made you feel like there were a lot of Gs [g-forces] there as he pulled out. If you'd have had to cut right at that time, you would have lost that.

DP: Do you feel that a zenith has been reached in Disney films, from the shorts through the features? Do you feel that there is one film that is the best? Some people see the shorts of the 1930s as having the most vitality. Others see *Snow White* as the zenith. I was just wondering, as an animator, if you felt that "Gee, we've never quite equaled that particular film?"

OJ: Well, I don't think we've ever equaled *Fantasia*. It's hard for me to say any one single one, because I think *Pinocchio*, having the fantasy and imagination that it has as a picture with a story, is hard to compare with one like *Fantasia*, where there is a different approach. But *Fantasia* was such a giant step in an entirely new direction and really so entertaining in its own way, that I almost have to say that is to me the peak, though I personally didn't enjoy working on it nearly as much as I have the ones with a story. But I'm flabbergasted when I look at it. And the music, the way Walt conceived it with the stereophonic sound. I could say that I can see why there is a cult of people that really are just crazy about the picture.

DP: It is amazing. Even people who are critical of it have to admit a certain admiration for the effort. I think most critics feel at worst it is uneven.

OJ: I'd agree with that. How it ever got made, really? I remember Walt back in the late 1940s; I was up in his office with some friends of mine that had the railroad hobby that he knew. We got to talking about

Fantasia, and Walt was saying, "God, we could never make another one like that." You don't have the staff any more, and you couldn't afford to make it.

DP: After you started here, has all of your work been on feature films?
OJ: No. I worked on *The Brave Little Tailor* [1938] and *The Pointer* [1939] and *The Practical Pig* [1939], and I think I worked on a Donald Duck picture. [He also worked on *Mickey's Surprise Party* (1939).] I worked some on *Song of the South* and *Peter and the Wolf* [1955], *Susie, the Little Blue Coupe* [1952] and "Little Toot" [from the feature *Melody Time* (1948)]. I worked in very few shorts, really. The last time I did a Mickey was for *The Mickey Mouse Club* show. I did a couple of the openings and closings.

DP: As Walt's interest moved away from shorts to the features, several people have written that Warner Bros. and Tex Avery and MGM and others started passing his shorts in popularity. Did you feel that way?
OJ: I think if Walt's interest had stayed on shorts, he would have surpassed anything anybody else would have done with his personality-type of animation. He'd done all that. Gee, he'd been doing them since in the 1920s. Look at the Aracuan bird [*The Three Caballeros*] and some of those things that we've done. He pops all over the place and you get three of him at once. Walt made the big jump from gags to personality stuff. That was it. He spent himself on the features.

DP: Did you like Bugs Bunny or other characters from Warner Bros. or other studios? Tex Avery?
OJ: Yeah, I used to get a kick out of them. I enjoyed the Tom and Jerrys and Woody Woodpecker or any of those. I still like to see them occasionally, but it's just not the kind that I would have picked out to do for myself. I like broad action, but I like it with a little more sincerity, I guess you'd say. I thought Harman-Ising was doing some interesting stuff for a while. They were somewhat like our Silly Symphonies. Some of the things they did had kind of a charm to them. And some of the early Bugs Bunnys I thought were good, and then it seemed like they kind of repeated themselves.

Marc Davis

Marc Davis was born on March 30, 1913, in Bakersfield, California. Marc's family followed his father's career in the oil fields and moved frequently. After high school, Marc attended the Kansas City Art Institute, the California School of Fine Arts in San Francisco, and the Otis Art Institute in Los Angeles before joining the Walt Disney Studios on December 2, 1935. He began as an apprentice animator on *Snow White* and served as a story sketch artist and character designer on *Bambi* and *Victory through Air Power*. Another of the Nine Old Men of Animation, Marc created some of the most memorable female characters, including Tinker Bell from *Peter Pan*, Maleficent from *Sleeping Beauty*, and Cruella De Vil from *101 Dalmatians*. Marc also animated on *Song of the South*, *The Adventures of Ichabod and Mr. Toad*, *Cinderella*, and *Alice in Wonderland* as well as shorts, including the acclaimed *Toot, Whistle, Plunk, and Boom* (1953). Marc transferred to WED and contributed to Disneyland's Enchanted Tiki Room, Jungle Cruise, It's a Small World, Pirates of the Caribbean, and Haunted Mansion. Marc retired in 1978 and was named a Disney Legend in 1989. He died in 2000.

I interviewed Marc on October 14, 1978, at his art-filled home in Los Angeles, which he shared with his wife, Alice, also a Disney Legend. They were very gracious and hospitable. We kept in touch through the years with the wonderful Christmas cards that Marc created each year. Their beloved dogs were frequently the theme of the cards. On my first visit, one of their dogs clamped down on my pants leg as I entered the house and I practically dragged the dog along with me to the site of our interview. But since the dog had only grasped material and not me, we became friends. Marc was a true giant in the animation world and his art touched and entertained so many and will continue to do so.

DP: How was Cruella De Vil different from other Disney villains?
MD: I think she was a combination of things, an attempt to do a villainess that would be fun rather than a villainess that would just be terrifying. You know, there were a lot of complaints about the witch in *Snow White*—and really with no qualifications, I thought. Then I did Maleficent, and she was just an evil character and had little or no personality, because all she did was make speeches. You have to have some kind of human contact with people. I think this is the beauty of Cruella, which I can't take responsibility for. This is Bill Peet's writing, putting together the story content. But making it work was a delight.

DP: I think she is probably the best part of the film—her bustling in, her whole movement. She has her own energy source.
MD: Christopher Finch spoke very well of that in *The Art of Walt Disney*, which pleased me, because I'd never have thought of the description that he wrote: half death-head mask and at the same time, a highly sophisticated fashion model type. ["Her face is a blend of death mask and fashion plate, perfectly expressing her character, which is at the same time evil and laughable."] But the angularity of the woman came quite honestly, probably because that was part of the way she was done. Also, she was reminiscent of several different people that I knew. I tried to get this—how would you say?—erratic thing in movement and personality and a thing that could flip from one side to the other.

DP: It is interesting, because even with the angular cheekbones and everything else, after initially seeing her, you accept her as a real character.

MD: She probably was a little inconsistent in drawing style with the other characters and a little more highly caricatured. I think this is one of the most difficult things in a cartoon, to keep a unity of all the characters when you have many different people, with different outlooks on drawing and styling and everything, putting characters together in one picture. It's very difficult.

DP: Someone wrote about the variations in the character design in *Cinderella*. The sisters were almost caricatures, while some of the other characters were more realistic.

MD: Well, again, that was different people working on them. This has always been a problem. It's always been a conflict amongst animators, too, and yet really, it's nobody's fault. It's just that no one person could control the animation in a whole film, because there's just too much to do. And certainly Walt Disney was the only man in the world who could put that many people together and have them turn out a feature film as consistent as it was and still have it work and be believable. He deserves full credit for putting that many different personalities together and having them not kill one another—you know, commit murder! Because there always were personality conflicts.

DP: With a group of artists, I imagine it's difficult.

MD: Well, strangely enough, the artists were sometimes less visibly temperamental than people in other areas. This always surprised me. Musicians were a little more apt to be upset than the artists, and so were a lot of other people in other areas, in a visible sense. Yet I think there was always the annoyance that you couldn't do the whole thing your way. The thing that always bothered you the most—particularly from the standpoint of being a key animator on a character—was that you didn't get to do the action. The action was generally done by somebody who had less talent and less ability, because it was less critical to the picture. Personality was the thing that your key animators had to do to make the picture come off. But doing the action was oftentimes a lot more fun and you rarely got the opportunity. The one picture I did get the opportunity was on *101 Dalmatians*. I did all of Cruella, so I can take credit for the good things and the bad things as well. There's some animation that if I had a chance to do it over, I would, but that's always true. I remember one time Frank Thomas saying—and I think this is true—"When you get down to about the last three scenes of a film, you know then how you should have done it."

DP: When you say a "key animator," I am not sure I understand exactly what you mean.

MD: A directing animator. One animator generally would supervise the animation of a character. In other words, Milt Kahl would supervise two or three characters. Maybe he'd help a lot of other people on their stuff, too. But he was the number one man, and every critical scene with the character he was involved with, he would be doing. The personality was the thing. I know this was always a problem, because [Milt] would be annoyed if somebody did a thing and it wasn't well thought out, wasn't well conceived, or was poorly done. He wasn't about to forgive them. And this was a feeling I think we all had, that you still had to work with some guys who just never would reach that point where they really understood what the thing was all about. But still they could contribute a certain amount of footage. The guys you appreciated the most would come to you for help on the drawing or the conception of a scene, the staging of a scene, or something else. Really, the directing animator had more control over this than the film director, who in most instances really was not a director in the sense of a live-action picture but rather a man who was kind of holding the thing together from all the technical points of view: timing out the footage, dialogue, making out exposure sheets, and so on. Yet still the directing animator would go up and make his suggestions, which generally a director would go along with, because you were giving something more thought than he would have had the opportunity or the capability to do. In the early days, an awful lot of directors came out of animation—they were expendable as animators— but still they knew the business and so they became directors. I wouldn't say this was 100 percent true—it wasn't—but in many cases, it was a man that Walt didn't quite know what to do with. And then there was also an ego factor that when a man became a director, he believed it.

DP: I think Ben Sharpsteen would probably fit that classification.
MD: Very much so.

DP: He says that Walt could have kicked him out. Instead, he made him a director. Maybe Wilfred Jackson would feel the same.
MD: Well, Wilfred was a very thorough man. He was so thorough he was kind of inclined to be a little pedantic. I know Walt kind of got bored with him in later years, so he always had Wilfred doing the opening of a picture and the ending of a picture for the simple reason that he knew it would work. He knew that Wilfred would introduce the characters, and they would work and so on. Then I think Wilfred reached a point where he became very annoyed with Walt. I was afraid at one time that he was going to have a nervous breakdown before he left. I'm not sure he didn't! Well, as I say, there are lots of personality things, and even when you talk about somebody, it doesn't mean that you don't admire them, because I admired Jackson tremendously.

DP: He is a wonderful guy.
MD: Terribly skilled person. But again, it's that overall personality thing, this many people having to work together. And when you first worked with Jackson, everything was spelled out, even to eye blinks. Then as he got to know you and he respected you, there was less of that. Then pretty soon, he realized that you could be pretty loose with what you did if you made it work and made it work better than what he had planned.

DP: Was there one director that you liked to work with the best on the short subjects?
MD: I don't know. I really got along pretty well with most of them. I didn't have any real problems with directors, I don't think, because I didn't permit myself to be in that position. Although I think at certain times, we all had kind of ups and downs with a certain director. Certain

directors were very loose and had not worked out things as well as they should have. In other words, we'd feel that they hadn't done their jobs. And then some might almost overdo it, like Jackson certainly did with younger people and newer people. As I say, this is just a matter of putting that many personalities together, especially in those days when we were doing those big features and there were so many in the animation department. I don't think I ever saw a film that Jackson was the director on that wasn't superb. And yet, always this conflict. Walt himself created a lot of his conflicts. As a matter of fact, Walt didn't like people working together who were too friendly, liked one another too much. He liked to put people together in conflict. He felt that he got a better job out of them. I never particularly agreed with him on that.

DP: It would seem to cause a little more tension, anyway.
MD: Yeah, and it's always that kind of upset. It was sometimes very annoying, especially in animation. Animation is something that demands such concentration and a dedication to hard work, because it certainly is hard work.

DP: I imagine. I'm in awe of people who can do anything like that.
MD: Well, number one, you had to be or should be a damn good artist. Number two is—and of course, a lot of these things are developed, too, when you move in with an organization like this, because you don't really know what talents you have in regards to that—to have a sense of entertainment, to have a sense of acting, to have a sense of comedy—all these things. Until you are put in a position to do something with it, you don't know whether you have it or not. And a lot never do. And some come up with surprising things. So it's a weird combination of talents.

DP: Kind of an actor and an artist?
MD: Actor, artist, and some sense of fun, some sense of humor, and knowing how to put this thing together for somebody else. You can take a good story and louse it up with bad staging and bad presentation. To be able to stage things clearly and make them work—this was the thing, of course, that Walt was the master of—taking and building a character.

There may be one big laugh at the end of this thing, but it came out of the development of the character and not because it was a mechanical gag in the sense of slapstick or something else. It was never the "Look, Ma, I'm dancing" type of humor. It was always a thing that built up through personality. I think if there is anything that's Disney, that's it as much as anything else.

DP: Regarding *Sleeping Beauty*, you have said that you felt the backgrounds were too busy and kind of stage sets.
MD: Yeah. That was again a conflict of personalities. This was Eyvind Earle, who does magnificent things, but he was so in love with his backgrounds that they didn't give you a good stage to stage business in because they were so busy. But Walt at that time was very intrigued with them. Also, this was the first time we had done a Cinemascope feature [*Lady and the Tramp* was actually the first Disney animated feature in Cinemascope], so he felt that this picture could be like moving illustrations. Well, we went ahead and animated a sequence, and it was pretty dull. This was Jackson. I animated on it. Walt came in. He felt with this big screen you could keep a scene on for a long time. But when he saw the sequence, he said, "For God's sake, don't you know there's such a thing as cutting? My God!" So then you began to realize you could cut in and around and you didn't pay any attention to this thing being wide. Our feeling was, when we first saw Cinemascope, that it was like looking through a mailbox slot, which was not true.

DP: Do you think that the story of *Sleeping Beauty* also hurt it?
MD: I think very much so. It was not one of our better efforts. It was terribly inconsistent. I never felt that the king sequence worked, although it was beautifully done by Milt. I never liked the backgrounds on it. I think his development of the characters was just great, but it was like all of a sudden having something happen in an aircraft hanger with three people. And it never came to life the way his animation should have. I blame this on direction, on background, and on the general staging of it. I felt personally that those characters were kind of inconsistent with the rest of the film, too. We had tried to create a very strong style for this,

which in some ways was good and in some ways, I think, was a mistake.
We went a little overboard on it. And I was one as responsible for it as
anybody else. Tom Oreb did some styling and they were just magnificent, beautiful drawings. And again, trying to get something that would
go with Eyvind's style of backgrounds, which I think to a degree they
do. Yet everybody wasn't able to design their characters and put them
into that same thing. So you had some characters that were pretty round
and roly-poly and others that were kind of severely designed—the girl,
probably Maleficent, and a few others. The animals were very severely
designed, and I think that was a mistake. And the girl was a mistake, too.
I think we were not equipped to make that kind of a graphic change at
that time.

DP: I think that it is a better picture than the initial criticism of it. It
doesn't seem to have the sympathy or the heart that *Snow White* has,
though.
MD: No.

DP: But that is built into the basic story, I guess.
MD: Again, it was the basic story. There wasn't that much you could
do about it, really. The story was such a simple one. Walt found such
a great angle on *Snow White* and the warmth of the characters, and I
guess maybe the naïveté of the times, too, had something to do with it. I
think we were a little too sophisticated by the time we got to this one to
develop characters and personalities that would interweave the way Walt
had done it on *Snow White*.

DP: I think that's a masterpiece.
MD: Well, it is. It's one of the greatest pieces of storytelling. I think it's
the best that Disney ever did, and I think it's one of the best of all time,
too.

DP: I really think it's as great as *Gone with the Wind*.
MD: I agree with you. And yet it has crude animation by comparison
with some of our later films. But everything worked. It worked from the

standpoint of personality and scene by scene. Of course, that musical score by Frank Churchill, and Larry Morey's lyrics (and others, I know, contributed to them)—just absolutely magnificent.

DP: When I see that picture, I think of what I've read and what people have told me about working at Disney's in the 1930s. It seems like the excitement from that period is in that film. I can feel it in *Snow White*.
MD: I started there at about the time that they were starting that picture. Walking to the studio from where I was in the annex across the street and then hearing some of this music being run just on the movieola—clickety-clack—I thought, "My God! What a privilege! I am listening to music that nobody on the outside has ever heard before." I was quite captivated by the music, but I think at the time that I had no realization how great it was. Certain musicals like *South Pacific* I don't think have a bad song in them. I think the same of *Snow White*. There was not a bad song in it. Every one was memorable. So anyway, this was one of the startling things in going to work there, hearing the music and then see-ing some of the first animation. I ended up working as an assistant ani-mator on the girl. They let each of us animate a scene when the picture was almost finished. This was meant as kind of a bonus. I can't even tell you which one I animated now!

DP: On another occasion, you talked about the changes between 1928 and 1935 and how much Disney had grown.
MD: Well, that was Walt. It couldn't be anybody else but him. Nobody really, I think at that time, had any comprehension of the fact that he was attempting to do a full-length cartoon. Everybody thought he was insane, just like they thought he was insane when he was going to do an amusement park. Only it wasn't an amusement park; it turned out to be something else. Even with all of the imitations, nobody else really under-stood what he had down there, nor was anybody else equipped with the staff that he had to fulfill it. That was again to his credit—the fact that he knew he had to get in better artists and he had to educate them to do what he wanted done. This is where Walt deserves such enormous credit, and he probably was making absolutely nothing. We were making

very little, too, at the same time, so it was kind of a group gamble in a way, although he was the one who was gambling. We were, as young artists, just lucky to be able to make a living in the art field. Even though we were paid what sounds like pennies today, at that time the economy was so different that you could get by. And a lot were not getting by until they got that job. A lot, including myself, didn't know particularly what this was all about. Still, Walt Disney was hiring artists. Then when you got in, you kind of took to it like a strange drug, and it became a competitive thing to see whether you were capable of competing. There were so many talented young people at the time, and there were good ones who were let go and some bad ones, I think, who were kept on. There had to be thousands who went through there, and Walt was very lucky that he was building the studio at that particular time. He couldn't start from scratch now the way he did then, because the economy just wouldn't permit it.

DP: The Great Depression was a help.

MD: Well, for him it was. For us, it was a time of great tension and tremendous strain. When you arrived, you had a tryout in an art class for a couple of weeks and then you learned how to inbetween, which was one way you could kind of earn your keep a little bit. Then if you could do that, you had demonstrated the ability to draw. Walt wanted to have people highly trained, so he brought in people to teach story, to talk about art, to talk about anything that he felt would make better films.

DP: I think I read somewhere that you looked out the window one day and you saw Albert Einstein walking through the studio.

MD: There were many of them. He just happened to be one who caused you to do a double take. But there was such an interest, so many people! It's hard for you to realize now, but of course, we didn't have television, and we didn't have too many picture magazines. Practically every magazine at that time—and these were the sophisticated ones like *Vanity Fair*—ran articles about this young genius, Walt Disney, and a picture of him as a very thin young man holding maybe a drawing or a doll or something else. What he had done somehow hit so strongly with the public in a time when if ever people needed a laugh or some relief, that was it. And you had radio and motion pictures. Motion pictures were very cheap to go to at the time; generally, they gave away prizes, like groceries and dishes. When Mickey Mouse appeared originally or when Pluto went howling across the screen, that just by itself was a riotous laugh. Unfortunately, there are a lot of people who are still doing that type of humor, and an awful lot of the cartoons that are being made for television are not that solid and not that funny. I think Walt recognized that there had to be more than that. When he finally did the *Three Little Pigs*, that thing just hit the country like wildfire. You have no idea the impact that that picture had and the impact that song, "Who's Afraid of the Big Bad Wolf?" had because everybody had the wolf at their door. I am sure he could not have had any conception of how that thing would hit. It made *Snow White* and everything else possible in its own way. That picture was made before I came there. I was living in Sacramento at the time. My father—I don't know how he happened to have dropped in and seen it—took me to see the *Three Little Pigs* at, I think, the old Alhambra Theater. That's all we saw. He was so intrigued with this picture, and I must say I was, too, but I still didn't think of it as a place for me to work. Then later, I was up in Marysville. My father had died, and I worked up there for a while. I did some work for a local theater over in Yuba City.

DP: What kind of work were you doing?

MD: Oh, I did posters, signs, advertising mastheads, and some things for a local newspaper. I also worked in a print shop. Somehow I managed to survive. I had had some sign experience previously in San Francisco after I ran out of money going to art school there.

DP: Did you grow up in San Francisco?

MD: No, I've grown up everywhere. I went to twenty-two different schools before I got through high school, so I had traveled a great deal. I think that a lot of that experience has a lot to do with my own creative background. I saw enough of life before I ever got to the studio that I wasn't out of one grammar school, out of one high school, out of one art school, and here I am ready to approach the world.

But getting back to Marysville, the man who owned the theater called me up and said, "Gee, there's a wonderful cartoon by Walt Disney over here and I think you ought to see it. You know, it's the kind of thing you might like to work in," or something like that. The cartoon was *Who Killed Cock Robin?* [1935]. And I must say I was just enormously impressed. I saw it three or four times. It struck me in a more personal way than the *Three Little Pigs*, and I began to think that I might like to work at Disney's. Around that time, I decided to come down to Los Angeles. I didn't think only of Disney. I wrote a letter to Disney, and I received a reply. I don't know how they made the mistake, but it began, "Dear Miss Davis, Sorry, at the present time we are not hiring women artists." I wish I'd kept the letter! I was sore and I dumped it in the trash and forgot all about Disney. Then I came down here and I thought I'd like to get into some form of motion picture artwork. I had a few contacts. But everybody was telling me, "Gee, Walt Disney is hiring. Why don't you go out there?" So finally I did, and I've been there practically ever since. As I say, once you got hooked, it was like a drug. The marvelous young guys there were from all over the country, and a lot of them were from all over the world. It was a terribly exciting time. It's awfully hard to describe because they were all young, all full of hell, all anxious to do something. None of them could understand what the hell we were doing, you know. And it took a long time. Now the animation has been done, and you can say, "Well, you do it this way and that way." The thing was that you just didn't really know what this thing was about; but the excitement was that every day, somebody did something that hadn't been done before. This was the excitement. This was the thing that excited Walt, and he began to see things materialize. And he was always asking for more. Once you learned how to do something very well, you were never asked to do that again. You were asked to do something else. This was a tremendous challenge that only a man like him would ask for. He was a man who visually, I guess you could say, to the public had to be the most conservative man in the world, but he was anything but conservative. He was a gambler, but he also believed in himself and he believed in what he wanted to do. It took a few years for him to gel in his mind what he wanted to do. And then sometimes he would go along and let us do some of the silly things that we wanted to do. Generally, they turned out pretty bad!

DP: I imagine that part of the excitement of that period would have come from having the opportunity to work closely with Walt.
MD: In the early days—the Hyperion days—I never had that much contact with Walt personally. He worked through his directors and key animators. He was moving like a bomb through the studio. I don't know how many people were there when I came in. I came in on December 2, 1935, and there were quite a few guys who were ahead of me: Ken Anderson, I guess, was there a year ahead; Milt Kahl was probably there a year ahead; Frank Thomas, Ollie [Johnston] and Eric Larson, maybe ahead of them; Woolie [Wolfgang Reitherman]; and of course, Les Clark, who was way ahead of any of us. So it took a long time for you to get any attention from Walt.

DP: What were your first impressions of him?
MD: We were all pretty much in awe of him, because after all, you could open up magazines and here were articles about this man. Also the fact that he could hire and fire you. You could never fully understand this man. I saw one Walt, somebody else saw another Walt. I'm sure Ben Sharpsteen had one, and Milt Kahl had another one. I think we—Milt and myself—were probably a little closer to the same Walt.

DP: What is the Walt that you saw? How would you characterize him?
MD: Well, it's hard to say. I really "met" Walt after *Snow White* was over. I worked on a couple of shorts as an assistant animator, and then I moved over to the *Bambi* unit, which was located across the street from the studio. Then we moved up to Hollywood to a place on Seward Street. We developed the story of *Bambi* there. I worked there primarily as a story sketch man. Walt didn't come over there very often. Finally the lease ran out at Seward Street about three months before the main studio opened up in Burbank, and they moved us out there. We were the first group to move into the studio. We moved into the 3-B wing. Then Walt began to see the drawings I had done, and apparently he was quite delighted with

them. He decided that I had to be an animator. He put me in with Milt and Frank, and he said, "Teach him how to animate. I want to see his drawings on the screen."

DP: That was a nice step up!
MD: Yes, that was a nice step up. So at about this time, Walt knew me and I began to know him. Walt had a lot of respect for me as an artist and for being knowledgeable about art, so I had some rapport in that area. As years went on, I had great contact with him in many, many areas. In later years, I had very close contact. But to have gotten his attention in the days when there had to be twenty-five or thirty guys coming in per week and maybe twenty-four of them leaving! He was not in a position to come over and say, "Oh, you're a nice-looking group" or something like that. That was a thing that he had set up an organization for—both good and bad. There was a guy at the head of it who was not a very bright man.

DP: George Drake?
MD: Yes. Not the most lovable character in the world, nor knowledgeable either. He was a rather nervous, ambitious guy, and I think he made a lot of mistakes. He made a lot of enemies for the studio, and he wasn't that well liked either. But still, within the limits of his personality, I guess you could say that he meant all right. But he did a lot of harm. He also was Ben Sharpsteen's brother-in-law. [He was actually a distant relative of Ben Sharpsteen.] That was one thing that hinged on a little bit of nepotism!

DP: He interested me, because Ben never talked about him.
MD: I think he was a great embarrassment to Ben as time went on. Don Graham, on the other hand, was just a marvelous man. He handled the study of art and the teaching of drawing. He gave a critical analysis of what he saw in the Disney films. He was a very warm man; so I think for somebody like myself who was terribly interested in art, Don Graham had more to do with my staying. Had it just been George, I think you'd have said, "I just can't tolerate this even though I need it desperately."

I think a lot would have gone—and of course, a lot did. A lot came through who were as talented as anybody who remained with Disney, and they still went off into other areas and they excelled. It wasn't for everybody. It took a particular kind of temperament, and it took being so fascinated with something that you just wanted to be a part of it. You wanted to excel at it, so you had to be ambitious.

DP: Also, I guess, to be able to work in a team situation.
MD: Yeah. That's something, too, because a lot of people are creative loners, and I must say that in some regards, I think I am too, thinking-wise. Still, the nature of this business was that it was only as good as the worst guy on a picture. If there was resentment amongst the top people, it was when somebody did not do a good job. When somebody did a good job and Walt complimented them or we saw it ourselves, God, you were delighted and you were thrilled for them. It was like being on a baseball team, and if a guy hits a home run, even if you don't like him, you love him at that moment because you win the game. This was invariably true. If Walt said, "Gee, so-and-so did a great thing," he probably wouldn't tell the person directly, but everybody else would say, "Hey, Walt said you did so-and-so. Gee. I'd sure love to see it! God, that's great!" and so on. This was a very high compliment, because Walt found it very difficult to compliment people directly to their face. He would say, "Yeah. Yeah, I like it." Well, bells rang and everything else. You felt good for a week. If there is a change in the organization from Walt's time to now, it's this: There is nobody there who could make me feel as good by saying, "I like that" as Walt.

DP: Nobody carries the weight.
MD: Yeah, they don't carry the weight. But there was something about that that you knew he meant what he said. You also knew that he was highly qualified.

DP: Did you work on the Ichabod part of *The Adventures of Ichabod and Mr. Toad*?
MD: No, I didn't work on that. I worked on an awful lot of them. I worked on *Song of the South*, *Cinderella*, *Sleeping Beauty*, and *Peter Pan*. I

did the original Tinker Bell in *Peter Pan* and the first animation that was done on her. And I worked on the Mr. Toad film [*The Wind in the Willows*, later part of *The Adventures of Ichabod and Mr. Toad*]. We worked on Mr. Toad during the strike. It was kind of a miserable time to be working on something of that sort, because there were so many things on your mind. It was the first thing that I did, after *Bambi*, where I was fully on my own as an animator. I did some good things and some bad things on it, I guess. Let's see what other pictures I worked on. I worked on *Alice* [*in Wonderland*].

DP: One list also included *So Dear to My Heart*.
MD: Yeah. I worked on story on *So Dear to My Heart*. Ken Anderson and I did the little stories that were in the scrapbook, but I did not animate on it. I worked on story on *Victory through Air Power*, and they neglected to give me a screen credit on it. I was sore as hell. I got an apology from Walt on it, because I did visually create an awful lot that was in the film.

DP: With the Disney Studio emphasizing personality animation and some of the other studios, like Warner Bros., going off in a different direction, did you ever feel that shorts coming from other studios surpassed the Disney shorts, or was it more like "We are doing one thing and they are doing something else"?
MD: More that, I think. I think we admired some of the early UPA cartoons very much, because we liked the freshness that they had. We mistakenly got hooked on some of that. It was inconsistent with our own capabilities or Walt's point of view. He did permit us to do a few kinds of avant-garde things and they were generally pretty bad.

DP: *Toot, Whistle, Plunk, and Boom*?
MD: Well, I worked on that, and it did win an Academy Award. It was fun to work on. I must say I enjoyed it. I worked on the one that was ahead of that, which was called *Melody*. I don't think Walt liked either of them. He tolerated them so that the guys could get it out of their systems. We did a duck picture [*Duck Pimples* (1943)] that Vip Partch did the story on [with Dick Shaw], and it was pretty bad. It was one of

those tongue-in-cheek things. Walt was never tongue-in-cheek, and I think our own development didn't permit it. It did with [Ward] Kimball, but Kimball was always kind of out on his own anyway. Kimball was always way over there. I think in a lot of instances, his animation was very inconsistent with the animation of other people in features. In later years, I don't think he tried to do anything but his own thing. I always felt that he was wrong in that. Yet he is one of the great talents— no question about that—an incredible draftsman and a fine animator. When he did something like *The Three Cabs* [*The Three Caballeros*], it had absolutely superb animation, surprising timing, amazing speed, and amazing ways of putting things together. But some of his work was very inconsistent with Walt's desire to bring something to life. When you began moving a shape around on the screen, you lost Walt, and also, I think, you lost our audience, because our audiences were so much more universal than the audiences for some of those other types of cartoons. UPA was great for the art houses, but they made very little money. I think the average person was not impressed. He would rather have seen Donald Duck squawk across the screen or one of our shorts like *The Clock Cleaners* [1937] or *Lonesome Ghosts* [1937], which had a story and some great humor. And there were many, many more great little films, a lot of which have been forgotten. They were based on telling a story and doing it with characters that you could believe in. At the time that *Snow White* was released, I asked a man who was about my father's age if he had seen the picture. "No," he said, "I don't like cartoons. I like things that are real." I think that this was something that Disney had: you brought something real to life, or if it wasn't real, you brought it to life anyway and you made people believe in it. The Bugs Bunny films were kind of a formula type of humor. They were well done for what they were. The Tom and Jerrys were also well done for what they were. A lot of the Harman and Ising cartoons were pretty artfully done. But Disney still had this one thing of developing character and bringing it to life, making you believe that this situation was real. It's so remarkable to have progressed from 1928 and a *Steamboat Willie* who just jumped up and down and squeaked to the brilliant *Snow White*, where you believed that these things came to life.

DP: Audiences crying over the "death" of Snow White.

MD: Right. You felt with the characters. The terror of Snow White running through the woods fleeing the huntsman—there was great emotion there. This is also true of the scenes when the witch finally finds her or when the dwarfs discover her. It was just a remarkable accomplishment for a man to have done in such a short length of time. Starting in a business where most of the men were comic strip artists animating *Mutt and Jeff* and similar films. These films were little fillers on a theater bill, along with a newsreel, a travelogue, or some type of film, and one feature. Of course, that all died. The Disney short died when there really wasn't a place for it anymore on the theater bill.

DP: With the advent of the double bill?

MD: Yes. The double bill just put them out of business, because the theaters wouldn't pay enough money. At the time, Walt was selling them through the RKO lease, and he was getting about fifty thousand dollars or fifty-two thousand dollars for a short. The cost was about fifty thousand dollars. He reached a point where he couldn't participate. When he didn't participate, they kind of went downhill.

DP: What about the other studios?

MD: I think that Warner Bros. was probably capable of turning out a short in one or two weeks. That was the competition that we couldn't meet, because they were not asking for the same level of quality. As I say, these things were awfully well done for what they were. They contained some clever things that we could not or would not do, because it was again inconsistent with Disney's type of storytelling.

DP: In Bob Thomas's book, *Walt Disney: An American Original*, you were credited with this quote from Walt Disney: "Dammit, I love it here, Marc. WED is just like the Hyperion Studio used to be in the years when we were always working on something new." Did you get that same feeling at WED?

MD: Yes. About six months before Walt died, he came in one day, and he just flopped down in a chair in my room. He said, "You know, Marc. I like to come over here. You know, just like the old studio." Well, he didn't say any more, and I interpreted it as saying that he liked to come over there because it was fresh. What was happening there was something new. He said of the studio, "These guys know how to do these films." I won't say that he lost interest in them, but he couldn't spend his time, because he added too much to the cost of them. These guys all knew how to animate, and they knew how to put a picture together pretty well. I do think a lot of the pictures suffered very much—and suffer still—by the lack of his attention. I think that the pictures are now talking themselves to death, whereas in his version of the pictures, you talked when you needed to talk, you acted when you needed to act, you had action when you needed action, and you used music when you needed music. But you never talked just to be talking, you never talked to be clever, and you never talked to make jokes. It was never the Bob Hope/Jack Benny type of humor nor the Fred Allen type of humor—standing up and making funny remarks. So at WED, we were doing things and finding better ways to do things. He was again demanding that we do more interesting things.

DP: I read about your trip with him to the New York World's Fair. That must have been quite an exciting thing to do.

MD: Exciting. Tense. To have been with this man for, say, ten hours straight was not the easiest thing in the world. For one thing, the man had practically total recall. He could remember something I had said three years before, and if I said something different, he'd call me on it. By that time, I must say, I had learned to be a little guarded in just not letting things roll off the top of my head and think I was going to be funny to him, because he wasn't a man who had a great deal of small talk. Yet this doesn't mean that he wasn't a very warm individual. He was a warm and a very generous guy in his own way. There was one image that he was looking for more than anything else, and this was his own. Going through the World's Fair with him was a marvelous experience and a very emotional one.

DP: Did you just visit the Disney-designed attractions?

MD: No, we went through a lot of things. We went through It's a Small World. When we went to the GE exhibit, I warned, "Well, now, look, don't expect too much out of this animation." "Why?" I said, "Well, it's kind of tired machinery. It's been here for two years, you know." He said, "Oh." We went in and sat in the back row. Together with Walt and myself were the guy who ran the pavilion and Bob Mathieson. He [became] one of the heads of Walt Disney World down in Florida. We went all the way through and when we came out, Walt said, "Hell, Marc! That doesn't look too bad!" But if I had said, "Oh, hell, it's great!" he'd have said, "Jesus Christ!" and so on. Then we went to the Miss Clairol exhibit, because we were thinking that they might be interested in coming into Disneyland. This exhibit was for women only practically, but we went through it anyway with the man who ran it. After seeing a few exhibits, we came into a room and there were quite a number of young girls there. They discovered Walt and they shouted, "Oh, Walt Disney! Walt Disney! Can I have your autograph, Mr. Disney?" I'd say he autographed maybe six or seven pieces of paper. Then a little girl came up wearing blue jeans, a sweatshirt, bobby socks, and tennis shoes. She said, "Oh, Mr. Disney, may I have your autograph?" He put his hands on her, and he said, "Look, honey, I just can't autograph any more. I'll be mobbed here." She started screaming, "He touched me! He touched me!" From there, we went over to IBM to see their show. I'm not sure we didn't go to other places in the meantime. They had kind of a traveling wall that you sat in and you went up in and saw the sights. Nobody seemed to pay any attention to him at all. Finally, we got up, and at some point, I don't remember exactly where, they all stood up and applauded. Then we went to the Scandinavian thing for lunch. It was very nice. He was pretty much left alone, but you'd see a few people noticing who he was. We finally ended up at the Ford exhibit—I think we skipped Lincoln—and they wanted to VIP him. But he said, "No, I want to go through the whole thing. I want to go through like the public." So the three of us, plus the man who ran the show and a couple of Ford managers went through the whole serpentine—

DP: Was this in the car?

MD: This was the long walk going in there. You're on your feet for a good half hour before you ever get up to those cars. There was that long serpentine line going back and forth that eventually lined you up with the exhibit car. In the line were a heavyset but well-dressed woman and a well-dressed man with a hat—typical New Yorker types. I saw them look at Walt. We serpentined so that we were next to them. This woman looked at Walt, then she looked back at her husband, and she said, "It isn't either!"

We finally got into a car. There must have been seven or eight hundred people there, and they broke into tremendous applause. But not one person looked at him. Typical New Yorkers! You wouldn't have known that they even recognized him until he got into the car. And I thought about that woman. I told Walt about her later, and he got a big kick out of it. After the exhibit, we went up to the VIP room for a drink. Then we went our separate ways, but we were together from about 9:30 in the morning until 6:00 at night. We saw a lot of different exhibits, many of them designed by other people. He wanted to see them, and he wanted to see them as the public saw them. He didn't want special treatment. In every instance, as I recall, he did that. He liked to do that sort of thing.

DP: I understand that he liked to do that at Disneyland as much as he could.

MD: Yeah, as much as he could. Of course, he was recognized there. I went through there a number of times with him, too, and it got a little testy, because he would sign a few autographs, and then all of a sudden, he would be mobbed. He was down there for other reasons, and he could not stand there like a guy in a bookstore autographing books all day. It wasn't that he didn't want to do it, but he knew when it was a good time to pull away from it. But he liked to be recognized. He was going to Europe one time, so he went up to the barbershop at the studio to get a haircut. He said, "Give me kind of a short haircut. I don't want to be recognized." So the barber said, "Sure, Walt. Why don't you let me shave off your moustache?" "No! No!" He didn't not want to be recognized that much!

DP: Was your last meeting with Walt very shortly before his death?

MD: About two weeks, I guess. I never saw him alive again. That is still a strange thing. He came in and he flopped down in a chair. He looked like the wrath of God. He was skinny. He was always saying that you had to take off some weight and that he had to take off some weight and so on. So I made a comment and I could have bit my tongue off for it. I said, "God, they sure knocked a helluva lot of weight off of you." He just looked at me with this thin face. Anyway, he saw the first drawings that I had done: a whole flock of this bear band [which eventually evolved from the Mineral King project into the Country Bear Jamboree], but many different versions from the final thing. God, he saw those, and he laughed like hell. He was very pleased with them all. Well, in the meantime, one of the executives came in. As soon as Walt came over, boy they had their spies out! "Oh, Walt's here!" He looked in at the door, and Walt kind of hit his stomach and said, "Look, I'm not here on business. I know you're a busy man, and you got a lot of things to do. I just want to talk to Marc." So then after about fifteen minutes, I began trying to figure out how I could entertain him more than this. So I said, "Well, we have the animation set up for the McDonnell-Douglas Flight to the Moon." After looking at that, I said, "Did you like it?" He said, "Oh, yeah. Yeah." By then, we had gathered maybe seven or eight people. He was there maybe ten minutes and then he turned to Dick Irvine and said, "Dick, I'm getting kind of tired. You want to drive me back to the studio?" We all kind of stayed back. I started toward my room, and as he went down the hall, he turned and said, "Good-bye Marc." He never, ever said good-bye to anybody. Whether he had some premonition or not, I don't know. But anyway, two weeks later, he was gone. It was a very touching thing. I think this whole business will wait in kind of a talent limbo until somebody else comes along who has that drive and says, "I'll risk everything on what I believe." I think this young [George] Lucas who made *Star Wars* and who is, I understand, a great Disney fan, took a tremendous gamble on making a live-action cartoon, and yet I have read that he said that he wanted to do it like Walt Disney would have done it had Walt Disney been doing it.

DP: Steven Spielberg, who made *Close Encounters of the Third Kind*, is also a big Disney fan.

MD: Well, I'm very pleased to see that they're bringing in a lot of people. I feel that when you don't have Walt, you should now give this thing a different look. Walt never hired big-name directors for his live-action films because he liked to direct them. He wanted people who would do what he wanted done. This was a thing from his early days.

DP: It was always his studio.

MD: Right. It took a long time to realize that he was hiring you to do what he wanted done. He wanted you to give him something to judge from, and he wanted the best you could do and then better than that.

Dave Hand

Dave Hand was born on January 23, 1900, in Plainfield New Jersey. He attended the Art Institute of Chicago before returning to the East Coast and beginning his career in animation at the J. R. Bray Studio. Hand later worked for Max Fleischer on the Out of the Inkwell series. He came to California to consider live-action filmmaking but returned to animation, this time with the Walt Disney Studios. He joined the staff in 1930, animating on more than forty shorts, including *The Chain Gang* (1930), *Traffic Troubles* (1931), and *Flowers and Trees*. He began directing in 1932 with *Trader Mickey* (1932) and continued as Walt Disney's first director on *Building a Building* (1933), *Pluto's Judgment Day* (1933), *Who Killed Cock Robin?* (1935), *Thru the Mirror* (1936), *Little Hiawatha* (1937), and many more. Walt assigned Dave to be supervising director of the studio's first animated feature, *Snow White and the Seven Dwarfs*. After that triumph, Dave performed the same role for *Bambi* and then served as animation supervisor on *Victory through Air Power* before leaving the studio for an animation opportunity in England. Dave died on October 11, 1986, and was named a Disney Legend in 1994.

An interesting aspect of memory is how each person remembers events differently. While Dave recalls accepting criticism from Walt at previews, whether deserving or not, Ben Sharpsteen, in *Working with Walt: Interviews with Disney Artists*, recalls Dave trying to flee from a disappointing preview early, only to be stopped by Walt as he attempted to leave the theater parking lot in his car.

I interviewed Dave Hand through correspondence dated September 7, 1979. He was hesitant to participate in a face-to-face interview, and as consequence of that reluctance and my budget constraints, I never met him in person. Needless to say, I wish I had.

DP: As a director of shorts and feature films, you worked closely with Walt Disney. Was it difficult for you to keep up with his innovations and experimentations? Was it difficult to follow his lead?
DH: No, it was not difficult for me to keep up with Walt Disney's innovations and experimentations. No, it was not difficult to follow his lead. Sometimes it was difficult for him to know just where he himself was going—he would be trying to get a handle on his dreams.

DP: How did you happen to go to work for Walt Disney?
DH: I left New York to go to Hollywood to look the live-action situation over. It didn't look so good, so I applied at Disney.

DP: What were your first impressions of Walt? Did they change over the years?
DH: My first impressions of Walt were that "he was always right." Even if I didn't think he was—but I had enlisted to learn his way of doing things, so I followed his wishes.

DP: As a supervising director of *Snow White*, did your approach vary greatly from the supervision or direction of shorts? In other words, how does one go about directing the first animated feature? Were you allowed much latitude, or did Walt monitor all that you did?

DH: No, my approach did not vary in my supervision of *Snow White*— there was simply greater scope. *Snow White* was really a group of shorts (which were sequences of *Snow White*), so the only added problem was to hold it all together as a unified whole. I was allowed full latitude on all details of production—Walt monitored the *results* from Story to Preview.

DP: As one of the "New York animators," was it difficult to adjust to the Disney approach to the production of animated cartoons?

DH: The only difficulty in "adjusting" to the Disney approach was that there was no acceptance of slipshod animation (as there had been in New York) and no thought of cost relative to quality.

DP: How did the Disney Studio compare to other animation studios where you have worked?

DH: I saw no difference in working at the Disney Studio except as noted above.

DP: I have heard several accounts of Walt's on-the-spot evaluations at previews of shorts that disappointed him. Did these sessions create a great deal of anxiety?

DH: Walt's evaluations at previews of shorts that disappointed him didn't bother me. I knew that those I directed had certain weaknesses, which were evident after a preview. If criticism came my way, I sat quietly and took it—whether it was justified or not.

DP: As one of the first directors in a constantly evolving medium, how did you coordinate the work of animators? As the art of animation became more sophisticated, did you supervise animators differently, or was your approach to direction basically the same?

DH: I think coordinating the work of animators took care of itself. All of us had complete dedication to Walt and the medium, and because of this we were all anxious to help each other get the very best results. As a director, I never thought I was in any way superior to the animator (and certainly did not act it). It was teamwork—animators helped animators, directors helped animators, and animators helped directors— total unity.

I always considered animators—each one separately—as marvelous human beings with wonderful ideas (some maybe not so good as others—the ideas, I mean) and always encouraged them not to take a scene until they were completely satisfied that it worked. And besides, they were all I had to "get it on the screen"!

I never changed my basis for directing—I only worked to get better at it.

DP: What was it like for you to work at the Disney Studio during the 1930s and early 1940s, the period historians generally regard as the Golden Age of Animation?

DH: For me, working at the Disney Studio was an intense twenty-four-hour-a-day experience, with ever-new challenges always over the horizon. The problem for me (and I suppose for all of us) was that there wasn't any way that we would know whether something was good or bad until the idea was shown to the theater audience (and then it was too late to correct—that is, if it were bad). There seemed always to be a struggle to make an idea work—from story to final animation approval. There just wasn't any way to positively know whether the idea was going to get over. It would be only through experience and a sixth sense (which Walt had in abundance) that could in a manner assure some measure of success. Even so, we weren't always right (including Walt) in the way we presented an idea.

Speaking only for myself, as I gained experience, I would never take an idea that I was responsible for putting on the screen (whether when I was an animator and later when I was a director) until I was satisfied that it would work. When I became a director, I encouraged my animators to do the same thing. When I was an animator, I would argue with the director until the idea was somehow changed so that I would be happy with it—and when I became a director, I would argue with the story men (including Walt) until the idea was acceptable to me. However much Walt fussed about my approach if his idea and mine didn't agree, I'm quite sure he secretly liked it. Why else did he select me to direct *Snow White*?

DP: On *Snow White*, animators were cast by characters, but on *Bambi*, the film was broken down by sequences, and any animator could animate any character. What kind of problems did these two approaches pose for you as the supervising director? Did you prefer one approach to the other?

DH: I don't think you have your conclusions altogether right about the casting of animators on either *Snow White* or *Bambi*. Animators were selected for their type (style) of animation. Those animators whose style seemed to be compatible with the particular character(s) would be given key scenes in order to establish (for all the animators) a basis for the personality of the character because the character would be used in many scenes (say) throughout the picture. All key men would confer back and forth about all characters, but usually one guy would be the "authority" on his character. This was the general plan, although sometimes it was altered. This would be my approach.

Walter Lantz

Walter Lantz was born on April 27, 1900, in New Rochelle, New York. He began his animation career at sixteen, working with Gregory La Cava at the studio set up by newspaper magnate William Randolph Hearst to create cartoons from popular comic strips. After two years, the studio closed, and Walter joined the J. R. Bray Studio. At Bray, Walter also worked as a producer, creating films that combined animation with live action with cartoon characters Dinky Doodle and Colonel Heeza Liar. But Hollywood beckoned, and Walter arrived in 1927, working first as a gag writer for Mack Sennett and then moving to Universal Studios, where he remained for most of the rest of his career. When Walt Disney lost the character Oswald the Lucky Rabbit to his distributor, Charles Mintz, Universal retained the copyright, and the company's head, Carl Laemmle Jr., soon asked Walter to replace Mintz as producer, giving Oswald a new lease on life and a new look under the other Walter. 1935, Walter Lantz Productions took the reins of animation at Universal and began producing cartoons under contract. Walter subsequently introduced many cartoon characters, including Andy Panda, but his most famous and most successful character was Woody Woodpecker, who had a huge box-office following,

inspired hit recordings of his theme song, spawned a vast array
of merchandise, and gave steady employment to Walter's wife,
Gracie, who succeeded Mel Blanc as the character's voice. Walter Lantz Productions continued to make short subjects longer
than any other major animation studio, but by 1972, even he had
to stop as a consequence of shrinking revenue from film exhibi-
tors. He died on March 22, 1994.

On April 23, 1979, two weeks after Walter received a
special lifetime achievement Oscar, I interviewed him in his
office, which was filled with memorabilia, especially of Woody
Woodpecker. He was friendly and forthright with his story and
opinions and I enjoyed meeting him, having been an avid fan
of his television show back in the late 1950s. I only wish he had
scheduled more time for our interview, because we were in the
middle of my questions when his next appointment arrived. But
I am happy to present what I was able to record with this true
pioneer of the animation world.

DP: How did you happen to get started in animation? I understand that
you went to work at the Bray Studio.
WL: Long before that. I really started in 1916. My first job was for William Randolph Hearst, who had started a cartoon studio.

DP: Hearst International?
WL: Hearst International, yeah. Cosmopolitan Pictures. It was set up by
a cartoonist named Gregory La Cava. I wasn't an animator; I was just
starting in the business—such characters that were famous in the Hearst
papers like the Katzenjammer Kids, Happy Hooligan, Jerry on the Job,
and all of those. We didn't create any new characters. That's where I
learned how to animate. When I was eighteen, I was an animator. From
there, I went to the Bray Studios. That was about 1922. I was at Bray
working with George Stallings, who was in charge. Then George left and
I took charge of the entire studio. I made those combination [live action
and animation] pictures. I guess it must have been about 1924. They talk

now about how combination animation is new. Gosh, I did it almost sixty years ago, because I've been producing with Universal now for fifty years.

DP: One article discusses using blow-up photographs as opposed to combining live action and animation. I haven't seen any of the films where the backgrounds are actually photographs of a room. Did that work fairly well? Was it very effective at the time?

WL: No. The way I did it, the cameraman would photograph me going through my action, pantomiming with an imaginary character, assuming that the character is only maybe a foot high. We'd shoot that action first. Then we would take the negative and take about every other frame and make an eight-by-ten bromide photograph of every one of them. Then I'd take these photographs and put them on my drawing board and animate on tissue paper over the photograph. For instance, if I had him in my hand—I'd pantomime the action in my hand—and then I'd place the Colonel Heeza Liar or Dinky Doodle—what I was doing at the time—in the hand. Then we'd ink and paint cels from the drawing. Then we'd photograph each one of those photographs with that particular cel. They were numbered. We'd have maybe two or three thousand of those in a picture. We developed them in racks of fifty at a time so the density would be the same. That's how it was done. That was the first method of combining characters. Before that, Max Fleischer combined himself in the Out of the Inkwell series, but that was something different. That was rear projection. But he never used the system. In fact, I was the first one to ever use this system.

DP: In a book I read, I thought what they were talking about, in addition to doing that, was to actually photograph a room to be used as a background and then use blow-ups of the photographs with the cartoon character—just by itself in the room.

WL: Oh, we'd do that, yeah. Now that was a still. Say we had a scene on the drawing board or in the room, then we'd make an eight-by-ten still of the room, just like a painted background. We'd animate and photograph the cels on that particular still.

DP: I've never seen any of those kinds of cartoons. Was that effective?
WL: Very effective. I made over a hundred of those at Bray. You see, I was with Bray for about five years. I went with him in 1922 and I came out here in 1927 and started with Universal in late 1927.

DP: From what I've read about him, Bray sounds like he was a marvelous person and an extraordinary talent.
WL: Did you ever see that film he made, I think it was called *Dreamy Bud*? I think he made it in 1914. He made a combination cartoon. He drew the character on every frame of film and colored it by hand.

DP: I have a question on Oswald the Lucky Rabbit. As I understand it, after Mintz had the character, about a year later, Universal took over the character, or did you take it over?
WL: There have been so many stories about that. Most of them are all false, you know. People write them, but they didn't know what they were talking about. What really happened: When I went to Universal in 1927, Disney had been producing Oswald the Lucky Rabbit for Universal. He came up with the character of the Mouse, and Universal didn't want any part of it. They said that mice wouldn't go. So he left, and you know what became of the Mouse. He could have bought out Universal. So Universal wanted to start their own cartoon department. Mintz had been animating Oswald the Lucky Rabbit. This was the black and white rabbit with the long ears. But Mintz didn't own the copyright. Universal always owned the copyright to Oswald the Lucky Rabbit. [Carl Laemmle, head of Universal] asked me if I would set up a cartoon studio for them. I'd had ten years' experiencing producing cartoons before I came out here, so I said I would, but providing I could redesign the rabbit. I made him a white rabbit, which is not the Disney rabbit at all. So I produced Oswald the Lucky Rabbit for Universal for ten years. Going back, I set up a whole department for them—built desks, I had a camera built, and everything. I had to start it from scratch. We had over a hundred people working in that department, because we were turning out one every two weeks. I think I produced over two hundred. Then later, in 1937, when I went independent, Universal was having financial troubles and couldn't

produce cartoons. They asked me if I would produce them independently. They would release them.

Universal assigned all the copyrights of all the characters I had created for them, including Oswald the Lucky Rabbit. I still maintain the copyright on Oswald the Lucky Rabbit.

DP: Did Mintz ever have a copyright on that, or was it always Universal?
WL: Always Universal owned the copyright. Universal got Mintz to make a few cartoons. I don't think they made very many—maybe half a dozen or so.

DP: I had noticed that there was quite a change in Oswald.
WL: Well, that was a true story. You know, one of those jerks that writes for that magazine [Walter did not identify the magazine]—it's a good magazine—made a statement that I really resented, and I wrote to the magazine. He said I swiped Oswald the Lucky Rabbit. It's such a ridiculous thing for him to say. He didn't know what the hell he was talking about. But that's a true story I just gave you.

DP: Another thing that I was curious about also in connection with Disney was something I read regarding a feature film that he was thinking about making during the war about gremlins. What I read was part of someone's doctorial dissertation. He said that, I think, you and several other studios had been planning short subjects dealing with gremlins, and I guess Roy Disney had called you and a few other studios and asked if you would make the short subjects, because they were going to make the feature. They never did make the feature. Was that kind of cooperation common among studios?
WL: No, but we were a friendly group. We had an association, the Animated Cartoon Association, just a group like [Leon] Schlesinger [of Warner Bros.], and [Fred] Quimby of MGM, and Disney, myself. We always cooperated with each other. It was a very friendly group.

DP: When I read that, I thought that was a pretty nice thing for people to do. I would have thought that it might have been more cutthroat.

WL: Oh, no. As far as I know, this has never been a cutthroat business. For instance, if an animator had come to me and said he wanted to go to work for Disney, I'd call up Walt and I'd say, "Walt, this fellow thinks he can do better with you." He'd say, "How much you paying him?" I'd tell him. He'd say, "I can't pay him any more than you're paying him." That was the end of it. But if you could get an increase going someplace else, okay, God bless you, go ahead. No, there was no pirating of help. We had a wonderful group, and we still have. I think that animated cartoonists are a wonderful group of people. It's too bad that these producers right now haven't got the money or the time to do the type of animation like we all did in the past. See, they're limited with time and budget, and that's why they call it limited animation. All these producers that are making cartoons today could produce full animation, but I don't think it will ever be done again unless it's for a feature. I stopped producing Woody Woodpecker and the other cartoons [seven] years ago. And the reason I did, I could see the writing on the wall. They were getting to be so expensive that there would be no chance at all of getting in syndication. Those cartoons cost at least eighty or eighty-five thousand dollars apiece to produce today. When I quit, I was getting up to forty-five thousand. I said, "Jeez, this can't go on forever. I'll be broke." Disney quit ten years before I did. MGM quit, and then Columbia and Paramount. I was the last one to throw in the sponge. But fortunately, by going independent, I own all my own cartoons. So we syndicate them. Oh, I have several hundred that have never been on television yet. So I feel very good about being able to play these cartoons on television, so that the present generation of young people can see what we did years ago.

DP: Certainly what you did years ago is better than the kind of thing that's being produced now.

WL: Especially see some of those musicals I made with forty-five-piece orchestras. Today, you couldn't even use a hand organ [laughs].

DP: I remember your television show. It was on in the 1950s, wasn't it *The Woody Woodpecker Show?*

WL: Yes, in 1957.

DP: You would come on and talk about animation.

WL: How animated cartoons were produced. Yeah.

DP: That was a long time ago for me, but I have a pretty good recollection of it, because I used to watch it all the time. In fact, I think one of the sponsors sold a Woody Woodpecker hat. I used to have one of those. I don't know how I ever let it slip through my hands.

WL: Yeah, that was a good show.

DP: I was about eight years old then, but I was really impressed with what you were doing on the show.

WL: It had never been done before either. Our show is doing very well now in syndication. We cover pretty much of the country. Although I am not producing, we reissue thirteen theatrical cartoons a year. We go back maybe ten years and pick out thirteen real good cartoons. They play in the theaters and the drive-ins. This generation has never seen them. So you see, with the types of pictures that I made over the years, I never produce anything timely or anything that would be any problem, you know.

DP: They don't become a fad, then.

WL: No. No fads. And that's why they'll be good in perpetuity, I hope.

DP: I wanted to ask you about Woody Woodpecker's voice. I was at a lecture given by Mel Blanc a couple of years ago. He mentioned something about having done the voice initially but then was under some kind of contract obligation, and you had to look around for another voice.

WL: Yeah, that's true. Mel did the voice for Woody for about four or five pictures. Then Warner Bros. signed him up to an exclusive contract, where he couldn't work for anybody else. He used to work for all of us. They signed him up, so I started shopping around, tried various voices. I decided on using Gracie, my wife, who had a lot of experience in the theater and was a good reader. It's a speeded-up voice anyway, you know. We shoot it straight up and then speed it up. She's been doing it now, oh, since 1950. That voice when you saw the presentation of the Oscar that I received, she did the bit that Woody spoke.

DP: Did any particular thoughts come to mind when you were getting the Oscar?

WL: No, except it was a wonderful feeling that after all these years in this business that someone in our field—fortunately, it happened to be me—was recognized. I felt really, as I said in my short speech, that I considered it as a tribute to the entire animated cartoon industry that produced all this creative art over the years. We've all given so much entertainment throughout the world, and we've never received the recognition that we should have received, especially from the theater owners. They still pay the same price for the rental of a cartoon they paid fifteen years ago. That's why we stopped producing cartoons, because we couldn't get our investment out of the theaters. Television is what saved us, really. This has been a wonderful industry. I'm so happy to know that this art is so appreciated. That ovation that I received at the academy—very heartwarming. That showed how much they appreciated not just my work, but they showed appreciation for really all the animated cartoons.

DP: They seemed to be really enjoying the clips, too.

WL: They'd never seen anything like that. That clip that you saw of me fighting the wolf, that was done about fifty-five or sixty years ago. Another thing that I'm very proud of: last year I took all this memorabilia that I had saved in warehouses. I sold my other studio and moved in here a year ago. I had all this material. It goes back fifty years. A lot of it was thrown out, but fortunately I saved enough. I had seven truckloads of it. I gave it all to UCLA. They, in turn, have cataloged all of it, and they have an animation archives there in my name. Anyone like yourself or any other students of animation can go there and look up this material. There are musical scores and backgrounds and animation and maybe three hundred thousand drawings or something—a lot of material. I feel very happy about that.

DP: That's great that you saved all that because that's all history. You know it'll be there forever.

WL: Yes. [If it was left] in a warehouse, when I pass on, it'd probably be lost somewhere [or someone would] forget it's there. I'm getting letters from people all over the country, congratulating me on receiving the Oscar. People I never knew. It's very rewarding to receive letters like this. Here's a picture sent to me, taken of Mia Farrow the night of the dinner. Came in this morning. She's a lovely girl.

DP: What was Robin Williams like?

WL: He's a very humble person. He's such a wacky guy at work, but he's a very humble person. Notice that when he was on the podium with me, he was a real gentleman. He was there, and he listened. Usually you get somebody that tries to take the whole thing away from you and tries to be real funny. A real gentleman.

DP: He's so fast with his humor.

WL: Oh, yeah. Oh, he threw me, you know. We had rehearsed the day before. When we went onstage, he didn't say anything we were supposed to say. I didn't have any cues or anything, so we just played it by ear, but it came off great. I mean, I think that's why it was so natural and looked so good.

DP: There was that one point when you said that Woody was here, and he said, "You mean he's not at Michael's Pub?" [a reference to Woody Allen].

WL: Well, that's what threw me, you know [laughs].

DP: I guess that's what comedians like to do. Do you feel that there is a division between those who control everything themselves, who create cartoons with a small staff, versus a large studio with many people all working on the same thing?

WL: I think it's really a division. These young people, sure, they're struggling in a sense, but they don't seem to come up with anything, with real humor. What I mean is, you take Bugs Bunny, Mickey Mouse, Popeye, Tom and Jerry, my cartoons, these characters all live and breathe. They think what they're doing. For instance, look at Tom and Jerry: they don't even speak a line. They have to do everything in pantomime. They're thinking. But the characters [current animators] produce, these way-out subjects—in fact,

the last ten years, I refused to even send a cartoon in to the academy. I've
received ten nominations, and I quit sending any more cartoons in, because
they were giving Oscars for a two-minute dirty joke. Then they were giving Academy Awards for [short] subjects that never saw the light of day in
a theater. They played in the art houses. And I couldn't see this. But they
don't have any, as I say, humor in these things. They're so cut-and-dried.
The characters are so ugly. They have no feeling in the characters. They're
very bad drawings. I don't even go the see them anymore. I'm an old-fashioned producer, really, because I like pratfalls and comedy.

When I first came out here from New York, I didn't know what I
was going to do. I drove out here and went to work for Mack Sennett
in the story department. He wanted certain animation done, and I did
it for him. I worked in the story department for three or four months,
before I went to Universal. I learned an awful lot from Sennett. If he
had a barrel of water and a body going to fall in, there'd be a label on it,
"Water." Dynamite was labeled "Dynamite," you know. I just believe in
a type of humor that's visual—nobody gets hurt, but it's funny. They're
striving for something. It's too bad. It's a lovely art. I don't know whether
it'll ever come back again, unless it comes back in features, where you
can afford to spend several million dollars to make a feature. We still
have a lot of talent in the business. There's a lot talent. This school
that Disney has out in Valencia—CalArts. They're doing a good job
out there. In fact, I give two scholarships a year there to two students.
They're developing some good animators, but as soon as they develop
them, they go right to Disney's, you see. I'm very happy. And Hanna-
Barbera is training people. But the thing is that they don't realize that
if an animator gets, say, two hundred dollars a week and he's doing full
animation, he can turn out 16 feet a week. If you give him four thousand
dollars a week, he still can only turn out 16 feet of that kind of animation. Now, that's simply arithmetic. I think that explains it to you, doesn't
it? Now, my animators never turned out more than 20 feet a week. Now
in limited animation, you'd have to turn out 180 feet a week. Let's take
a pose. The mouth will move in four drawings, and they time it to read
a whole paragraph of dialogue. But we acted out the dialogue. We used
arm action, body action, and everything else.

Gilles "Frenchy" de Trémaudan

Very little seems to be known about Gilles "Frenchy" de Trémaudan. He was born in Saskatchewan, Canada, of French descent. He attended the Otis Art Institute in Los Angeles, where he was a classmate of Wilfred Jackson (whose interview appears in *Working with Walt: Interviews with Disney Artists*). De Trémaudan was hired by Walt Disney and became an animator as well as a story man and sketch artist. He animated through most of the 1930s at Disney on short subjects, among them *The Picnic* (1930), *Pioneer Days* (1930), *Frolicking Fish* (1930), *The Birthday Party* (1931), *Traffic Troubles* (1931), *Mickey Steps Out* (1931), *The Barnyard Broadcast* (1931), *The Bird Store* (1932), *Flowers and Trees* (1932), *King Neptune* (1932), *Just Dogs* (1932), *Bugs in Love* (1932), and *Babes in the Woods* (1932). He married an inker named Doris while at the Disney Studio, but the marriage apparently lasted only a couple of years. He also became an American citizen during his tenure at Disney. He later worked at UPA. Two sources indicate that he became a monk and was apparently known as Brother Gilles at the Santa Barbara Mission.

Disney colleague Lou Debeny remembered Frenchy as a "super guy." Disney historian J. B. Kaufman shared this story from Jack Kinney:

was fine; we got along fine together. Frenchy was a very arty type of guy—he liked the classics in music, and he liked all the French artists and whatnot, and he liked all that sort of thing. He was a very sharp guy along those lines. See, we had a conglomeration of various types of people, all thrown together, which made things very interesting. Because on the other side of me was Johnny Cannon, who was just the opposite. Johnny was more sports-minded, and smoked cigars, and was entirely different than Frenchy. But that was good, that was what made the place come off—you had a variety of temperaments all thrown together. We fought, you know, we argued—and we laughed.

I interviewed Frenchy at the Veterans' Home in Yountville, California, on April 2, 1977. I had written to him but had not heard back, so uncharacteristically on impulse, I stopped in unannounced and asked to see him. He was in very poor health at the time and I was immediately sorry that I had pressed the point. But he said, "Since you're here, you might as well tape something." So we sat in the library and recorded the brief interview that follows. As I looked around at others who were also struggling through their final years, Frenchy noticed and said, "Well, this isn't Disneyland." My visit with Frenchy was one of my saddest experiences, but when I read the interview, I appreciate the warmth and the humor that shine through.

FDT: I was born in Saskatchewan, Canada, which is supposed to be an exaggerated state like Texas. I was naturalized American in Los Angeles. I was always proud of that. While I was at the Disney Studios, I became a naturalized American. I'm a Canadian-born Frenchman. They butcher the French around here [the Veterans' Home] all the time. I've met some of the boys that were in World War I. Some of their "trench French" is terrible.

DP: You were telling me earlier that you and Wilfred Jackson attended the same art school?
FDT: Otis Art Institute.

DP: Did Wilfred Jackson call you to come to the Disney Studio initially?

FDT: Yeah. The interview was by Walt. I was always proud of the fact that Walt Disney was going back east to New York on some cartoon business, and before he left, he phoned, I think it was Jackson, and he told him to hire me. In those days, Walt used to do the interviews.

DP: What was he like?

FDT: He was a tough driver.

DP: Did you like him in spite of that?

FDT: Oh, yeah. We used to call him Uncle Walt, but he was more like a father. He had a funny sense of humor. Some of the books don't credit him with much humor, but he had a keen wit.

DP: Did he play practical jokes?

FDT: He used to be the victim of jokes. We had a guy named Rudy Zamora, and Rudy was always clowning around. One morning, he had on a bandmaster's outfit. He marched up and down the hallway. All of a sudden, he turned a corner of the hallway and walked right into Walt. Walt told him to come up to his office and bring his animation. So Rudy Zamora went up to the office with a stack of the animation paper, but he only had two drawings completed, so he put one on the bottom and one on the top. He handed the stack of drawings to Walt. But Walt crossed him up. Walt took the paper and flipped through them and all he saw was this one drawing at the bottom and one at the top! So he was fired. Well, Walt later made fun of that situation on TV, so I guess he wasn't completely disgusted.

DP: You said before we started that you didn't like UPA very much when you went there?

FDT: Well, I didn't like the politics. I mean, I couldn't warm up to [Mr.] Magoo. I was a Mickey Mouse man, although I animated practically all of the early characters. I also was a gagman and story man and sketch man.

DP: Did you work with Roy Williams?

FDT: Oh, boy. Some of the stories he told us—I wonder how he survived some of them. He worked out pretty well as a clown with the Mouseketeers. Roy was an unusual gagman. I see where he is credited with thinking up the idea of the Mickey Mouse hat. Roy got the idea from an animated drawing of Mickey tipping the top of his head [*The Karnival Kid*, 1929]. In the early days, there was no limit, like Mickey would pull his spinal column out and he'd use it for a sword, but Ben Sharpsteen helped bring things within [reason]. Walt Disney's logic was if a chair had legs and if it had life, it would dance. Or even a piano stool. We kept within human boundaries. Marcellite [Garner] was one of my first girl friends, although I never dated her. But we used to ride to the studio together. I kidded Marcellite. I'll have to tell you the joke since you might publish this. Marcellite lived in Los Gatos [California] for a while. I told Marcellite, "So there you are, Minnie Mouse. I told you if you weren't careful, you'd end up in the cats!" meaning Los Gatos [Spanish for "the cats"].

Once Walt opened the door and a can full of banana peelings fell on him. That was another gag where he didn't think it was very funny. They tell about the early days of Walt when he worked on Oswald [the Lucky Rabbit]. The doctor told him to keep away from cigarettes. So one morning they found the garden hose throughout the building from Walt's animation desk. At the other end of the garden hose he put a cigarette. When people asked him, "What's the big idea?" he said, "Well, the doctor told me to keep away from cigarettes." So who says that Walt Disney didn't have a sense of humor?

Lance Nolley

Lance Nolley hailed from Texas. After a stint as a newspaper artist, he was working as a commercial artist in Dallas when he received the call to come to the Disney Studios. He joined the staff right after work was completed on *Snow White*. Lance has credits as an art director on *Fantasia* and *The Reluctant Dragon*; on story for *Fun and Fancy Free*, *Football Now and Then* (1953), *Paul Bunyan* (1958), *The Saga of Windwagon Smith* (1961), *The Litterbug* (1961), and several *Disneyland* episodes; and as a layout artist on *Make Mine Music*, *Melody Time*, *The Adventures of Ichabod and Mr. Toad*, *Cinderella*, *Alice in Wonderland*, *Peter Pan*, *Lady and the Tramp*, and many short subjects. At Hanna-Barbera, Lance worked as a layout artist on *Quick Draw McGraw*, *The Huckleberry Hound Show*, *The Yogi Bear Show*, *The Flintstones*, and several other television shows. He served as a production designer on *Bon Voyage, Charlie Brown (and Don't Come Back)* in 1980.

Lance was not an easy person to locate. Dick Huemer tracked Lance down for me through the union, and I interviewed him at his home in Burbank on August 11, 1978. Lance had not been in the spotlight very much, and it was a pleasure to talk with someone who had not polished his stories over the

years. He very generously shared his artwork, including a preliminary layout sketch from *Pinocchio*, with me. He was a big-
hearted Texan and I was so happy to have had the opportunity
to get to know him.

LN: At the time I went to work for Disney, they were in a rather desperate need for artists. There was actually a shortage of artists, and they were
combing the country. They found me in Dallas, Texas. We corresponded
back and forth. This is back in 1937. They offered me a job, and I accepted
and came out here towards the last of 1937.

DP: Towards the end of *Snow White*?
LN: Well, they had just finished *Snow White*. I got out here in time for
the premiere out in Beverly Hills.

DP: What were you doing before you came to Disney?
LN: I was a newspaper artist. I worked on the *New York Herald Tribune*,
and I worked for the Associated Press, and then things got kind of bad
during the depression, so I came home to Texas. I was doing commercial
art then, trying to work with different studios in the Dallas area, and I
was getting along fairly well, but then Disney saw some of my artwork,
and they wrote to me and asked me if I would like to go to work for
them. As I say, I accepted and I came out then. They had just finished
Snow White, and not to repeat myself, but I was at the premiere. They
gave everyone tickets—all the employees—and I got to see it. It was an
affair, believe me—tremendous.

[Starting work at Disney] like everyone else, you'd go to school
for three months in training and were taught by different animators.
Don Graham was head of the teaching class then. Actually, most of the
drawing at that time was design and life drawing. The human figure,
as Don used to say, is the basis of all art, so we studied that. Then I got
into animation. I was Norm Ferguson's assistant. Now, for your information, Norm Ferguson was the man who developed Pluto right from
the ground up. He made a real dog out of him. And so I was honored

to be his assistant. His drawing was so rough that I didn't have any trouble following it! I didn't have to draw too clean. So at any rate, after that, I became a little disenchanted with my progress in animation, and through Charlie Philippi, I got into layout and started on the next feature, which was *Pinocchio*. Then I worked on all the features: as I can remember, *Fantasia*, *Bambi*, *Cinderella*. [Lance worked on almost all of the features through *Lady and the Tramp*, but I cannot find a credit for him on *Bambi*.] I worked with them up to I think about 1960 and went over to Hanna-Barbera on *The Flintstones*. I stayed there about ten years, and then I retired. I'd had enough. But you know, I went back there last December and worked for six months at Hanna-Barbera. They don't do *The Flintstones* there anymore. It was all sent overseas to Australia. I worked on those, what we'd call adventure pictures, like *Godzilla*, *Captain Caveman and the Teenager*, *Scooby Doo*. I worked on those sorts of things. And finally I'll tell you, that's such doggone hard work. It was really hard and tedious. It took a lot of concentration. I just had to give it up and go back to playing golf.

DP: When you went from Disney to Hanna-Barbera, was that quite a contrast?
LN: Yes, it was. Every studio works a little differently, but basically, it all has to go through the same—more or less—process of story to layout to animation. I worked in layout with a chap named Richard Bickenbach. That's quite a name, but he was a fine man and a great artist. He's retired now. So I had good training. If you can draw, basically you can handle it.

DP: But as far as say the attitude towards the films or degree of perfectionism, was there a big difference between Disney and Hanna-Barbera?
LN: Yes, some, but Joe Barbera was a perfectionist. You had to please Joe in your layout. Bill Hanna handled all of the animation. He was the director of the animation, the whole bit, and Joe handled story and layout. But if we had a particular question in layout concerning the design say of a prehistoric automobile, we'd go to Joe, and he'd work very closely with us. He was a very fine designer himself, and he had a great story mind. No question about it.

DP: The reason I ask about Hanna-Barbera is that they are often regarded as somewhat of a factory-type operation, or at least not of the same quality as Disney. I was wondering if you found it to be that way.

LN: No, they try for perfection, as close as they can, but they have a tremendous program, a tremendous program. It is an insatiable appetite, this animation at H and B. You simply can't fill it up. There is always a demand for more artists, and frankly, all of the key artists, key animators at Hanna-Barbera, were Disney-trained men. All of them. There's Volus Jones, Bill Kyle, and a number of other fellows who were Disney-trained, and they grew up in that thing. So actually, pressure will bother anybody, but it will bother a Disney man less, because he's been through it all those years. It was a transition, I'll tell you.

DP: It wasn't necessarily going from good to bad or anything like that?

LN: No, no, because, you see, actually Hanna and Barbera are the two men who kept us all in the cartoon business by cutting down costs. Now on *Sleeping Beauty*, there is some animation in that picture that cost as high as two hundred dollars a foot, and that's prohibitive with the average studio. Walt Disney, the Disney people, always had enough money that they could experiment and get perfection. No other studio had that kind of money that they could spend months or years perfecting a character or perfecting a story.

DP: I guess Hanna-Barbera was under more pressure with television schedules—

LN: Yes. After the animation and the inbetweens are done, then it reverts back to the same system as any other studio—Disney and all the rest of them—of ink and paint, background painting. Background painters at Hanna-Barbera develop their own style, and of course, on *The Flintstones* it was a prehistoric approach. Actually it was fun to work on. It was a lot of fun to draw that stuff.

DP: I think *The Flintstones* was pretty clever.

LN: Yes. There was one man besides Joe Barbera, a fellow named Dan Gordon, who designed *The Flintstones* characters and a lot of the backgrounds, the different props, and so forth. He was a very clever man. He has passed away. He had a brother, George Gordon, who worked mostly at UPA on the [Mr.] Magoo series, as I remember.

But as we go along, we look back at the years at Disney, and I tell you, Disney, there's no question, was one of our modern geniuses. No question about it. And if you worked with him, he demanded perfection. He was a perfectionist. You might think it's perfect, but Walt had another idea. But he always knew what he wanted, and he could tell you. Now, if they know what they want and they can tell you, you can do it, but if you're always groping and trying to find the solution to the thing without help, it's difficult. But Walt could walk in and he had that sixth sense of knowing what would go in a story and also what the public would appreciate. He had that. I think he must have had that from the very beginning, even as far back as *Steamboat Willie*. I think that Walt could look at a story and tell whether or not it was going to go. He's the only man I've ever known who could do that.

DP: Somebody was saying that you would show him a storyboard and while you would be explaining, he'd be already picking out something.
LN: Right, way ahead of you.

DP: I was going to ask you what you thought of him as an individual, because I am fascinated with him. He's such a complex person. Everybody has a slightly different image of Walt Disney.
LN: Yes, well, that almost answers it. He was complex, and he was hard to understand, but I tell you, if you pleased him, he would reward you. He was fair. I say this: that anyone who worked for the Disney Studio, if they had anything on the ball at all, they would eventually get to show it or get to try. They were given a chance at Disney's. If you wanted to be a story man, a layout man, an animator, you'd get your chance. If you could fulfill the bill, why, you were on, you were a member of the staff. If you said, "Oh, well, I'm here in the Disney Studio, I haven't got a chance in the world, I'm too far down the ladder," but if you had an idea and you wanted to present it, you'd get a chance to show if you could do something. And that's fair enough. Nobody could ask for a better chance than that.

DP: Do you remember the first time you met Walt Disney?

LN: Yes, I do. I remember the first time I met him. I was working on *Pinocchio* and he was in the next room going over another picture with a man named T[hornton]. Hee. [Walt was saying,] "Now let's do it this way, and this one, pan down here." T. Hee yelled to me, "Lance, would you make up a sketch of this," and he explained to me what Walt had just said. So I did, and I took it in, handed it to the director, and he went in and showed Walt. This was my first experience with Walt. I was a little nervous, I can tell you. Walt said, "Well, that's not bad, but we're not going to do it that way." I was crestfallen, and the whole thing went out the window then. I thought I had done something that might be accepted, but he wasn't blunt or anything like that. He was very kind. He said, "Well, there's another way we can do it, so let's do it this way." I had actually, in my drawing, not interpreted his idea the way he was putting it over, so I just missed. But he wasn't unkind about it or belligerent. He just went right ahead with the story and laid my sketch aside, and then he made another little rough of more what he wanted, and we went right on. That was my first experience.

Well, I had a sort of a Texas drawl in those days, and Walt had a lot of fun out of it. I didn't take it personally. If I would tell a story, I'd say, "You all do this" or "They're gonna do this" or "Over yonder." I'd go along and Walt would sit there patiently, go through the whole thing with me, and then after it was all over, he'd say, "Well, sho' nuff!" I felt a little taken aback, but I knew that he was kidding. It was his way of having fun. So he was a fine man. When he passed away, actually I felt like—I wasn't working there, I was over at Hanna-Barbera—but you know, I felt very sad. I felt like I had lost a real close friend. However, we were never real close friends. I talked to Walt from a standpoint of man to man, and he liked that. He liked the approach of you being able to tell him in your way so he could understand what you were after, what you were trying to do. But he was a charming man to the public. When a stranger or a visitor came through the studio and Walt met them, he could be the most charming man. He wasn't always that way. In a story meeting or a layout meeting, he was right straight out. I wouldn't say he was tough or mean, but he knew what he wanted, and he would say what he wanted. Sometimes he'd use pretty strong words in trying to get his point over.

DP: I was wondering if you had experienced the Disney wrath that I have heard about from different people—that he was really good at telling off somebody if he really was upset with them. Is that what you are talking about at the story conferences?

LN: Oh, yes. I remember one time, one man in particular wasn't pleased with the way Walt was criticizing his work, and he just said, "Well, Walt, it just doesn't seem like I'm able to please you." Walt said, "Well, if you don't think you can please me, maybe we'd get along better without each other." And that's all there was to it. That was his way of dismissing the man, and the fellow knew it. That was the end of it. Walt didn't use strong language; he just told him.

There were a lot of very funny situations and cases. Walt smoked a lot, a heavy smoker. Ken Anderson, a fine artist and a great fellow, was one of Walt's favorites as far as presenting and drawing, because this guy could really do it. But one time in a sweatbox, Walt had a cigarette and he was reaching for a match. Ken was sitting on his right, and Ken smoked also. He lit his lighter and held it over for Walt to get a light, but Walt was looking this way, to the left, and the lighter came in right under his nose. When Walt turned back, it damn near set his moustache on fire! Walt let out a yell, "What the hell you trying to do? Trying to set me on fire?" And of course, the whole sweatbox, we had to stuff our fists in our mouths to keep from screaming out loud. Well, naturally, Ken was embarrassed to tears. Another time, Joe Rinaldi, who was a hell of an artist and a great story man, was working with Ed Penner on *Lady and the Tramp*. The boards were just perfectly drawn by Joe Rinaldi. One noon hour—Joe had been celebrating a little the night before, and he had a long ways to drive back and forth to Malibu—so he laid down. We had the storyboards slanted up against the wall. Joe crawled in behind them to lie down and take a little nap. This is on the noon hour, but before he could get out, boom, in came Walt and Ed Penner and several other people—the animators—and they sat down and started going over the boards. Joe couldn't come out! He had to lay there that whole meeting until they were gone. Oh, he was a funny guy, but he could draw like nobody's business. Joe Rinaldi and Bill Peet were two of the finest sketch men, and Tom Oreb, too. They could draw directly—directly. They never erased. What they put down stayed, and I tell you, that's something when you can take a pencil and lay it down and draw what you want to without having to go back and change it—directly. They were great.

DP: What was your reaction to the studio strike?

LN: Oh, that was a terrible thing, terrible thing. I wasn't a member of the union. Art Babbitt sort of headed that part of it—the strikers. I didn't go out. I stayed inside, but it was a terrible thing. We had to ride through that picket line, and they would holler, yell obscenities at us, and what they thought of us. I had a yellow automobile, [and they would say,] "There goes the yellow man in the yellow car." I mean, friends—we were good friends. Well, the studio, of course, is over it now, but it left a mark. It left scars. Friends who used to be friends. The government settled the thing, and they would swap a striker for a nonstriker, in and out like that. I got called outside. But I was very fortunate. I went to work for Walter Lantz. I worked for him about six months, and then I think Hal Adelquist called me at home and asked if I wanted to come back to the [Disney] studio.

DP: So you were part of the settlement when they laid off one nonstriker—

LN: Yes. Swap a striker for an inside man.

DP: That must have been terrible for them to lose people that they wanted because of the settlement.

LN: Yes. When I came back to the studio, Ben Sharpsteen greeted me and shook hands with me and told me, "Well, now, we're awful glad to have you back." And I said, "Well, of course, I'm glad to be back."

DP: Working in layouts and art direction, did you find that the freedom you had varied depending on who the director was?

LN: Yes. You mean the approach that we would take depended on the director?

DP: Yeah. When the storyboards came down, as I understand it, the director and the layout man would get together.
LN: Yes, that's right.

DP: Would some directors want to control everything themselves, and would others give you more freedom in your layouts?
LN: Right. That's very true.

DP: I don't know which directors you worked with, but what were they like?
LN: Well, the fun man who would just turn you loose and let you go your way and depend on your good sense of drawing and ability was Jack Kinney. Now, Jack Kinney directed practically all of those "How to do" [shorts] with the Goof—you know, like *How to Play Baseball*. He knew what he wanted, and he had animators like John Sibley, who was a fun animator. He could take a situation and make it funny, no matter what it was, by his animation and by his drawing and design of the characters. Wilfred [Jackson] was a little more thorough. His approach was a very serious approach, that everything depended now on how we're going to do this. He would go over the layouts very carefully, and usually you'd even thumbnail in a layout before you made a final drawing and showed it to him. He would approve it or make some changes. He was a very thorough worker.

DP: Did you work with Ben Sharpsteen?
LN: Yes. But at the time that I worked for Ben Sharpsteen, he was more or less a supervisor or associate producer, I would say, in that capacity.

DP: Did you find him difficult to work with or easy to work with?
LN: Well, Ben was a disciplinarian. He wanted you to come to work at eight o'clock, go to lunch at twelve, be back at one, and quit at five. He wanted you to sit there and work. That's fair. I mean, you came there to work, so you should, and he didn't want any horsing around. He wanted

the work done, and you produced it, put out, turned out, in the best manner that you could. He was fair. He didn't have a happy disposition. He was pretty serious all the time, very serious about everything.

DP: Did you work with any directors? Was Dave Hand there, or was he gone?

LN: Dave Hand was there when I first got there, but he was gone not too long after I got there—a year or a couple of years later. Gerry Geronimi—I worked with him.

DP: How was he to work with?

LN: He was good. Gerry was a little hot-tempered. You know—he wasn't temperamental; he just had a temper. But he was a good director. He was a damn good director. He was a good timer: he knew how to time the stuff, and he knew what he wanted. God, if they know what they want—

DP: I imagine there would be nothing worse than somebody hoping that by giving you a vague description you're going to come up with what they want when they really don't know what they want.

LN: Well, yeah, let you animate it and then see if that's what they want. Now, if they don't, you've got to do it over. Of course, story and layout's a different thing. They can watch it as it goes along, but animation, if they hand it out and it's all timed, then for an animator to go through it and rough it—that's why at Disney's, I believe, actually they saved money by roughing it and then pencil testing it and then letting the director see it or let Walt see it. Then if they have to change it, you haven't lost too much. But at Hanna-Barbera, you draw direct. Every drawing you make is *the* drawing. That's the last drawing you're going to make on that character. So it was a difference.

DP: Would there ever be a case where you might work with another layout man on a layout, or generally does a layout man do his own specific sequence?

LN: Well, in my case, yes. I worked with Don DaGradi and several other layout men if it was a big picture.

DP: Did you work with Ken O'Connor?

LN: I worked for Ken as his assistant. He's a good man. He was a great one for perspective. Ken O'Connor's a perfectionist on that. Architectural design of any kind, he could handle that. I worked as his assistant for several years. I learned a lot from Ken. He taught me quite a bit in my approach to layouts. Ken Anderson was [another] amazing man. He was completely paralyzed. [He had] strokes.

DP: Ken Anderson? I didn't know that.

LN: He had a stroke on his right side. He was swimming, and it hit him on his left side. He recovered almost 100 percent. He went back to work and designed and drew [story]boards. He is very careful about his health. If he gains even three-quarters of a pound over the weight that he has set for himself, boy, he'll go on a crash diet right now to get rid of it. But he was completely incapacitated. He couldn't walk. He couldn't talk. He couldn't do anything. And how he ever made it out of there, I'll never know. Determination. He's always been that way. Just determined. But he was always tight, real tight, too.

DP: I noticed in *The Art of Animation*, by Bob Thomas, that you are listed as an art director on *Fantasia*, a story man on *Fun and Fancy Free*, and then a layout man on all the others. At that time, were you trying to find your niche or—

LN: Well, really I got into layout. I was trained by Hugh Hennesy, who was one of the finest layout men that ever existed in the business. He'd take a little bitty stub of a pencil, and—boy, this guy was a genius, absolute genius.

DP: Are there any outstanding memories of any of the films on which you worked?

LN: I tell you, the film that I thought was one of the best they've ever made and one that I really enjoyed working on was *Lady and the Tramp*. [And I was an art director on] *Fantasia*.

DP: Did you work on "The Pastoral"?

LN: Yes, "The Pastoral." And story, *Fun and Fancy Free*; layout, *Make Mine Music*, *Melody Time*, *The Adventures of Ichabod and Mr. Toad*, *Cinderella*, *Alice in Wonderland*, *Peter Pan*, *Lady and the Tramp*. Well, after all this was over, I became a story man again.

DP: Which films did you work on in story?
LN: I worked on the hookups. I did *Paul Bunyan* and *[The Saga of] Wind-wagon Smith*. Then I did the bridges of the Goofy pictures [for television]. Goofy would start out, and we'd interject in there *How to Play Baseball*, and we'd have to make bridges so that it would all run smooth. This was a hell of a job. An art director could be a layout man in my case.

DP: Did you work on any films that you didn't particularly enjoy working on?
LN: Yes. I loved *Pinocchio*. That was a great thing. *Cinderella* was good. *Alice in Wonderland*—I didn't particularly like that because, I don't know, they just could never seem to hook it all up to me. It just was so jumpy. Actually, when it finally got on the screen, it wasn't too bad. I enjoyed it then. But in working on it, it was a little difficult. I enjoyed working on all the shorts. I particularly enjoyed working on Pluto pictures. Nick Nichols directed them. I did most of the stories and layout. I worked on both that time. He finished the story, and then I'd lay it out. That was a fun deal.

DP: On *Pinocchio*, do you remember what your layout sequences were?
LN: I worked on nearly all of the fox and cat stuff. That particular shot that I gave you, they were going up the road. I think the cat was hiding around the post [in] that wall there. That wasn't the final layout. That was a sketch to set it up for the approval of Hugh Hennesy. He was a great man. That man drew with such ease. He'd take a piece of pan paper and a five-field pen, take a little stub pencil, and he'd start drawing. That paper'd just roll by. He'd fill it up. He was a genius.

DP: Do you think there's one particular feature that's the best as far as the art of animation?

LN: One feature in there that I thought was the best? I still think *Lady and the Tramp*. There are so many little spots that I think back over. It was a fun picture. The design was never difficult. It was a nostalgic thing; you didn't have to just make it up. You could go back and get references on the type of houses, the streets, stores, everything. *Sleeping Beauty* to me was too cold. No warmth in the picture anywhere. The background painter who designed that stuff, Eyvind Earle—God, he was a great painter! It was a masterpiece as far as color and all that, but you never warmed up. But I guess it made money.

DP: It eventually made money.

LN: Yeah, everything they've ever made is in the black now. Reissuing them. They wait five years [seven years at that time]. What a great thing they have. Every five [seven] years is another generation. They just reissue them.

Xavier (X) Atencio

Xavier (X) Atencio was born on September 4, 1919, in Walsenburg, Colorado. He moved to Los Angeles in 1937 to attend the Chouinard Art Institute. He began his career at the Walt Disney Studios in 1938 as an inbetweener on *Pinocchio*. He became an assistant to Wolfgang Reitherman on *Fantasia* and *Dumbo* before leaving for four years of service in the U.S. Army Air Corps during World War II. He returned to the studio and worked on short subjects, including *Toot, Whistle, Plunk, and Boom* and the innovative *Jack and Old Mac* (1956), *Noah's Ark* (1959), and *A Symposium on Popular Songs* (1962), which he and Bill Justice were instrumental in creating. The team of Atencio and Justice also created innovative titles for *The Shaggy Dog* (1959), *The Parent Trap* (1961), and *Babes in Toyland* (1961) and created the special effects for the memorable scene in *Mary Poppins* where the nursery is magically tidied up. X moved to WED in 1965 and worked on many attractions there, most notably writing the lyrics for "Yo Ho (A Pirate's Life for Me)" for the Pirates of the Caribbean and "Grim Grinning Ghosts" for the Haunted Mansion. X retired in 1984 and was named a Disney Legend in 1996.

I interviewed X at WED Enterprises on October 12, 1978, immediately before I interviewed Bill Justice. As an ardent fan of *The Mickey Mouse Club*, I enjoyed seeing some of the artwork on the walls of his office. As we were saying good-bye outside his office, he introduced me to Herb Ryman, who I was able to interview a couple of days later on this same trip to southern California. (On this four-day trip, I had the opportunity to interview X and Bill, Larry Clemmons, Ken Anderson, Marc Davis, and Herb Ryman!) I have seen X over the years at various events, most recently at the D23 Expo in September 2009, and he is always warm and kind and a great representative of the Walt Disney Company. Had I known that the *Pirates of the Caribbean* Disney attraction would spawn blockbuster films, I might have dug a little deeper into X's involvement with the song and the attraction.

DP: How did you happen to go to work for Disney?

XA: I was born and raised in Colorado. I came out right after high school to California, and I wanted to get into the cartoon business. I had an aunt whose husband was a musician on Scrappy cartoons [at] the [Charles] Mintz Studio. He said he could probably get me a job. So I came out. He took me over to Mintz. I hadn't any formal art training at that time. They were interested in the few drawings I had in my portfolio, but they thought it would be better if I went to art school for a little while. So they suggested I go to Chouinard's, which had a preanimation course at that time. So I went to Chouinard's. We had two teachers there who were also teaching night classes at the [Disney] studio, Gene Fleury and Palmer Schoppe. At the end of the semester, they asked us to get a portfolio together that they would take out to the studio to be critiqued by the animators: Freddy Moore, Ward Kimball, Ben [Sharpsteen]—all those guys. I said, "Well, no, I'm not interested. I'm kind of committed to go over to Mintz, you know. I'm not interested." Schoppe kept after me. He said, "Well, come on, get this portfolio together. At least you'll get a good critique." So I threw some things together into a portfolio, and they took them over to the studio. This was at the end of the school term, and I had thought, "Well, I'll go over to Disney's and see if I can get a job, a summer job, in Traffic and then go back to school." By that time, I was into the school part of it. So I went over to the studio, and in the meantime, they had called my home to come out for an interview. So our messages crossed. When I got there, I ran into two or three of the other fellows from Chouinard's there and wondered what they were doing. "Oh, well, there [go] my chances of getting a job now that these guys are looking for work, too." Then I was called into George Drake's office, and he said, "We called your home, and we want to know if you'd like to come to work for us." I was living in Hollywood at the time, about three miles from the studio at Hyperion, and I ran all the way home! I didn't even wait for a bus or anything! I got there breathlessly [yelling], "I got a job at Disney's!" So that was the beginning of my career at the Disney Studios. We started in a class, a tryout class, for a month's tryout. At the end of that time, why, they'd selected some of us, and some they didn't. There were fellows from all over the country that applied.

DP: How many do you think there were in your class?
XA: I would say about fifteen.

DP: And how many of them would they have chosen?
XA: They probably took about ten, I guess. And I'm the last one!

DP: Well, it was a good choice!
XA: Vip Partch was in that group, and George Baker of *Sad Sack* fame was in that group. So we had some good talent.

DP: Was Walt Kelly—
XA: Walt was ahead of me. He had already gone through that routine, I guess.

DP: It is interesting to me, all the cartoonists who came in at Disney's. Hank Ketchum was there.
XA: Hank Ketchum came right after I did.

DP: You have no regrets about missing Scrappy, I take it?

XA: No, that was the end of my thoughts. I don't know, I guess subconsciously I just felt that my chances of getting a job at Disney's were nil. I guess the fact that I had this contact in this uncle-in-law, that I just didn't think too much about Disney's at that point in time. I probably would have later on.

DP: And if you had gone to Mintz, you would have been going to the enemy! Were you an assistant animator then?

XA: I started out as an inbetweener. This training class was just before *Pinocchio*. After doing the routine of bouncing-ball tests and flag-waving and things like that, they put us on production. I went to work with Woolie Reitherman as an inbetweener. Bill Justice was his first assistant. He'd been there a year or so before me. So I started on *Pinocchio* as an inbetweener and then went into assistant [work] after that picture on *Fantasia*. So I worked as an assistant to Woolie Reitherman then on *Fantasia* and on *Dumbo*. Then the war came, and off I went to fight the nation's battle! I was gone four years in the service and then came back. The picture at the studio had changed quite a bit then; [it] had slowed down economically, and there wasn't the advancement that there had been prior to that time. I thought, "Well, if I'd have stayed and hadn't had to go off to war, why, I could have advanced quicker," but that didn't bother me. It was so enjoyable working for the Disney organization, no matter what capacity.

DP: That's what it seems like to me. Can you recall your first meeting with Walt Disney? Or I suppose your first contact with him?

XA: One of my early memorable contacts—you'd see Walt all the time, you know—but one day at the new studio here, I was standing at the elevator waiting to go upstairs, and Walt came up. Every time you'd see him in the hall, you'd say, "Hi, Walt." He'd say, "Hiya." This day, he came up to the elevator, and I said, "Hi, Walt," and he said, "Hi, X." He knows my name! I practically dropped to my knees and kissed his feet. I was so thrilled, here's this great man [who] knows my name. I could just relive that moment with you; [just as] vividly [as] the day it happened. Such a great impression.

DP: How long had you been there?

XA: I didn't have any contact with Walt at Hyperion at all other than just saying hi, and this was at the new studio, so this was probably two or three years. I found out later that he knew people, you know, but trying to recall everybody's name at the spur of the moment like that was pretty rough.

DP: I suppose everybody was involved in the strike one way or another.

XA: I went out on strike. I was Woolie's assistant, as I said, at the time, a young kid of twenty years old. They said, "Well, we're going to have a strike." "Okay, we're going to have a strike." They said, "It'll be over right away." So I went out. I told Woolie, "Well, all my friends are going out. I can't stay in, you know." "Well, do what you want. Do what you have to do." So I went out. But the strike lasted the whole summer. At the end of the summer, the end of the strike, Hal Adelquist, who was the personnel guy at the time, called me [and told me] that the strike had been settled and that they were taking some of them back. So he called me to go back to work. In the meantime, I had just got my draft notice, and I said, "Well, I'll see you in a year's time, Hal. Save my place for me." Well, it turned out it was four years later that I came back. So I missed the things that probably went on at the studio—you know, the bad feelings that were created by those who stayed in and those who went out, because some of those guys took it pretty damn seriously. I couldn't. We weren't supposed to fraternize, but I'd be carrying my picket sign and Woolie'd come out the main gate in his convertible. I'd stick my sign in the back of his car, and we'd go out to lunch together. Some of these radical guys would jump up, "You can't do that! You're not supposed to fraternize with those guys."

DP: The Art Babbitt followers?

XA: Yeah. Well, then after the war, I came back, and Art Babbitt had to be hired back according to the terms of the contract because he had been in the service, too. Then they asked me if I would mind being Art's assistant. I said, "No, I have no feelings about it one way or the other." So I was his assistant. I think the terms of the contract with him [were that] they had to keep him for a year. So at the end of the year's time, why, then he was let go, and then I went on to other assistant-type work.

DP: Did you find there was any stigma attached to having been out on strike?

XA: No. As I say, by the time I came back, everything had calmed down. As I understood from some of the other fellows, there were some awful bad feelings. But I never felt that I was deprived of any advancements or anything by the mere fact that I had been out on strike. Some of the guys who'd been out—for instance, Ken Peterson, who was one of the active people in the strike, he had a position of importance. So I think it was just a few individuals that bore a grudge. But Walt's feelings—I'm sure he must have been very hurt at the time by guys like Babbitt who went out. Babbitt was one of those people who was always fostering a cause, you know, no matter what it was. So this must have been awfully hard on Walt. But to me, being very young and not understanding things too well at that point in time, I went out because it seemed like kind of a lark. I had no family, no obligations. Some of the fellows that were out who were married had a rough time. But to me, if I'd go down and get the union welfare and enough to make my car payment, that's all I cared about. So it was a different situation. I wasn't a radical type. The guys that went out and formed UPA, they were radical at the time.

DP: I guess the time you missed was a time of making mainly training films and a lot of things that were a way of keeping the studio surviving.

XA: Yeah. They got the War Department contracts to do films and things like that, so I guess they were operating on a pretty tight shoe-string. Even after I got back, there were lean times. For instance, I came back as an assistant to the position I had left. So they couldn't touch me for a year. But in the meantime, when we finished a pic-ture—I can't remember which one it was—everybody was demoted. Well, not everybody, but animators were demoted to assistants and assistants to inbetweeners, etc. After my year's grace, why, then I was touched, and I had to go back down to being a breakdown [man], an inbetweener for a short period.

DP: Was that just for financial reasons?

XA: Yeah. So if they didn't have a picture going through right off, why, they'd just—they did fire quite a few guys at the time. And the industry, I guess—other than Disney's—operates that way today. Like Hanna-Barbera, they have these big schedules, and the kids work their butts off for three or four months, and then while their TV commitments are met, everybody is laid off. It generally comes around Christmastime, which is one of those unfortunate things. But they've learned to live with it some-how. It's rather unfortunate, because I don't think the animation [pay] scale has risen to that point where, like live action, a guy makes enough money on a live-action picture that he can afford to live on nothing for a few months. But in the animation business, they don't do that, so these kids fall on hard times. Some of those people that were in the business when I came and are still there are just professional inbetweeners or professional assistants who never had the ability to really go any further than that, and they're still doing the same thing. They seem to be content with it.

DP: When you came back after the war, did you work on the short sub-jects that were still being made, or did you work on the features?

XA: I worked on *Lady and the Tramp* as an assistant. Then I was mostly on short subjects. I was working with Jack Kinney then, who was a director on the Goofy short subjects. So I was the key clean up man on the Goof. I'd just key the drawings for all the animators, and then they had their own assistants who would follow them up. So I did that for several years after the war. Then I worked with Ward Kimball on *Melody* and *Toot, Whistle, Plunk, and Boom*. That's where I got my first screen credit on my first animation.

DP: An Academy Award winner.

XA: Yeah. That was a great picture. Then after that, Bill Justice and I teamed up, and we started doing crazy little pictures: *Jack and Old Mac, Noah's Ark, Symposium on Popular Songs*. Two were nominated for Acad-emy Awards. We got beat out by [John] Hubley [*Moonbird*] on one of them [*Noah's Ark*] and I don't know who else [*The Hole* by the Hubleys] on the other one [*A Symposium on Popular Songs*]. *Noah's Ark* was all stop-motion animation. *A Symposium on Popular Songs* was a combination of cartoon animation and stop-motion. [Ludwig] von Drake was in that. It was not really a new approach—they did stop-motion back way back in Walt's first days in the animation business—but he was intrigued by it. The fact that Bill and I ventured forth and did something fresh intrigued him, and he supported us. We did these pictures, and I think they were successful. We showed *A Symposium* here the other day to the younger fellows that hadn't seen it. They were rather intrigued by it.

DP: I understand that the Sherman Brothers had written some special songs for that, takeoffs on different songs.
XA: Yeah. These were parodies on the styles. They did a ragtime song called "Rudabaga Rag."

DP: They had one that sounded like Bing Crosby.
XA: They had a Crosby and a Rudy Vallee type—

DP: Did the work on these cartoons lead into the special titles that you did for *The Shaggy Dog*?
XA: Yeah.

DP: When you do titles, is that pretty much up to you how you are going to do it, or is it carefully structured as a cartoon would be?
XA: We storyboard it just as we would a regular cartoon. You take your elements. You know how many titles you have and how you're going to get from one to the other and use a character. I think *The Shaggy Dog* was the first one we did—how we'd wipe off one with the dog animating through, back and forth.

DP: Do you plan that yourself, or does that come from the story department?
XA: No, we were our own story department. We took the whole thing from the beginning to end. Bill was a very good animator on it. I did the styling and layout on that, and Bill did the directing and animation on it.

Bill has an uncanny sense of timing and phrasing. An animator with less experience than Bill would have a character mouthing the action and no phrasing of the head. This is very difficult in that type of animation in that you have to animate straight ahead. It's not doing two extremes and then going back and putting your inbetweens in. You know that at a certain time, you've got to be over here. On your exposure sheet, you have, say, a twelve beat. Well, exposure number one is here and then when you get down to twelve, he's got to be in this position. So you've got to move him there and just anticipate him getting to that point, instead of working back in regular animation where you just put your drawings in between. It's a lot easier. And then remembering where you were is another thing. If you have two or three characters, we'd have to work closely together and work out a pattern. We started on top and worked clockwise around the scene here, so you remember that you made a move on each one of these characters. You just don't go around and move them haphazardly, because you never remember, "Well, did I move that one or not?" And if you forget, did I or didn't I, you just say, well, we'll scrap it and start all over again, because there's no sense in proceeding if you can't remember, and if you're going to have a jump in it, why, it will have to be done over anyway.

DP: I was thinking as you were talking about that, it seems to me from some of the things I read about Walt Disney that using stick-figure type of movement or cutouts was about the stage animation was in when he started back in Kansas City. So it was probably nostalgic for him.
XA: I think it was, because he kind of sparked to it when we proposed it.

DP: I had a question concerning the Disney short subjects and the short subjects of other studios. Some articles I have read have suggested that the studio led in short subjects through the 1930s but then went into features and started paying less attention to short subjects. Other studios started to supersede Disney in the sense that they took the Disney style and went beyond it, either with emotions that weren't in Disney films, such as in *Bacall to Arms* with the wolf lusting over a Lauren Bacall–type character or doing the kind of impossible gags that Tex Avery specialized in. Other articles have talked about Disney's emphasis on personality animation in contrast to many of the other studios. Do you feel that either of these ideas is accurate?

XA: Yeah. As a matter of fact, we discussed it at the studio at the time. MGM was doing the cat-and-mouse films, Tom and Jerry, and they went into the slapstick part. We had been doing more than the cute personality stuff, the little fat bunnies, as we called it. Ward Kimball was chafing at the bit to get into some stylized animation as we finally did in *Toot, Whistle, Plunk, and Boom*. UPA was winning all the Academy Awards with their stylized cartoons. I asked Walt point-blank one day. I said, "Walt, how come you don't do any of those stylized things?" He said, "Oh, hell, X, they're making pictures for the so-called intellects, and I'm doing them for the heart. There's a hell of a lot more hearts than there are so-called intellects." I couldn't argue with that point! So that was his remark. As a matter of fact, when we did *Toot, Whistle, Plunk, and Boom* and won the Academy Award, he never really claimed it as his picture. [He said,] "That's Kimball's picture." I'm sure he was happy that we got the award on it, but it was still not his type of animation.

DP: Closer to UPA?

XA: Yeah. So we took what UPA had done and refined it. Now you have it to the point where Hanna-Barbera does the limited animation thing. Sometimes you run across one that's got some nice styling in it, but mostly the character is designed for full animation, and it is done in limited animation, and it just doesn't come across.

DP: So you would feel then that it was not a question of one being better than the other, it was just a different approach.

XA: Just a different approach. And as you say, we'd gotten into the feature business, so I think as a result, the short subjects suffered to the point that they weren't making the money. My understanding is that they weren't justifying the expense of making the cartoons. It had gotten so damn expensive to do a short subject that they finally decided they couldn't afford to make them anymore. That's why Walt let us go on these pictures that Bill and I did, because they were two-

reelers—featurettes as they called them—and they could be released as
a package with a feature, and they could make money on them. At that
time, they weren't making any more six-minute short subjects. They were
just giveaways, you know.

DP: Pretty much every studio ended up having to do that. I am interested
in the move from the studio to here. When did you come over to WED?
XA: That was right after we finished *A Symposium on Popular Songs*. Bill
and I then kind of split. We had done these things and we had done a
lot of things for *The Mickey Mouse Club*, including the opening "Mickey
Mouse March." No, we finished *Mary Poppins*. I guess that was our last
picture together, Bill and I.

DP: You worked on the nursery scene?
XA: We did the tidying up of the nursery scene, all the stop-action stuff.
Yeah. Then I went to work in Woolie's unit again, in the story depart-
ment this time. I did story sketch on *Winnie the Pooh and the Blustery
Day* and things like that. Then we started another picture that had
combined cartoon animation and stop-motion. It just wasn't coming off.
The Sherman Brothers had some songs for it. So Walt decided not to do
it. T[hornton]. Hee, I think, was working with us at the time on it, too.
Walt said, "No, I don't think I'll do it. I've been wanting to get you over
to WED for a long time." His interests were over here pretty much at
that time. We'd ask for a meeting [in animation], and we couldn't get him
for two or three weeks. Come to find out after I came here why, because
he was spending all his time over here. So they sent me over here. I'd
been on the main lot about twenty-seven years at that time, so this was
kind of a hard transition, then. As a matter of fact, driving home past
the studio, I'd actually get tears in my eyes. And I'd go back every day for
lunch. In a couple of weeks' time, [after] I got my feet wet here—and of
course, I knew most of the people here anyway—and got into a project,
why, I started weaning myself away from the studio, and I'd go back
every other day, and then once a week, and then once a month, until I
got to the point where I seldom went there unless I had something to do
there—a recording session or working with the film editor or something

like that. But after I came here, why, this felt again as the studio was
when I first went to work in 1938: a small little group and so many different things to do here—opportunities. For the first assignment I got from
Walt, after I had worked around with the model shop—Claude Coats
and the guys—he asked me to do the dialogue script for the pirate ride
[Pirates of the Caribbean]. God, I've never done scripts like that before.
Of course, I didn't say that to Walt. I knew damn well he knew what I
could do. So I scripted one scene of the pirate ride and sent it over to him
for his approval. He called me by phone and said, "See, I told you could
do it." That was it. I just went ahead. I'd pick up *Treasure Island* and books
like that to get the feeling of the jargon. "Alas there, matey!" So that's how
I started writing, and then I've been doing mostly writing since I've been
here. I did a song for the pirate ride, you know, just an idea. I thought the
Sherman Brothers or George Bruns or somebody could do it.

DP: "Yo ho, yo ho—"
XA: Yeah. I kind of sang a little bit to Walt one day when he was here. He
said, "Hey, that's great!" Have George put some music to it. So that was
it. I became a songwriter!

DP: That sounds exciting.
XA: Yeah. So it was all these little things, little opportunities that were
offered here, again reminded me so much of the early days at the studio,
the Hyperion days.

DP: I imagine wherever you were, if he were interested in what you were
working on, it would make it or break it. It would be exciting if he cared,
and if he didn't, it would not be quite the same.
XA: Yeah.

DP: I was looking through one of *The Mickey Mouse Club* annuals that
were compiled from *The Mickey Mouse Club Magazine* and I noticed that
you had done some of the illustrations. When the club was on the air, was
that something that would just be an extra assignment or something?
XA: Yeah.

DP: You mentioned that you are working on the Epcot (Experimental Prototype Community of Tomorrow) Showcase for Walt Disney World.

XA: Currently, I have worked on the Transportation Pavilion that will be sponsored by General Motors. Ray Bradbury and I worked together on the Spaceship Earth. On the World Showcase, I've worked on the Mexican Pavilion. I did a concept. And now we are getting down to the nitty-gritty. Even though these concepts were done a couple of years ago, we've got to get down to it. We've got to face it! The next four years are going to be hectic around here. [Epcot opened on October 1, 1982.] I think in essence it is an exciting project. But we keep vacillating; we keep getting away from the original theme, which is discouraging to me. That's one of our big problems in working with industry: we not only have to please ourselves, but we have to please somebody else. When we make a motion picture, we please ourselves and hope that it pleases an audience. First of all, it's got to be entertaining. That's what our media is, entertainment. And if we can teach while we're entertaining, well, great! That's marvelous. That was always Walt's philosophy: Entertain them, and if you can teach them something while you're entertaining, well, then fine. But don't teach and hope to hell you can entertain them.

Bill Justice

Bill Justice was born on February 9, 1914, in Dayton, Ohio. After studying at the John Herron Art Institute in Indianapolis, Bill joined the Walt Disney Studios in 1937. Bill animated on such Disney classics as *Fantasia, Bambi, Saludos Amigos, Victory through Air Power, The Three Caballeros, Make Mine Music, Alice in Wonderland,* and *Peter Pan.* Bill is also well known for his animation of Chip 'n Dale, stars of many short subjects.

Bill directed several experimental films, including *Noah's Ark, A Symposium on Popular Songs,* and *The Truth about Mother Goose* (1963). With X Atencio and T. Hee, Bill employed stop-motion technique for segments of *The Shaggy Dog, Babes in Toyland, The Parent Trap, Bon Voyage* (1962), and *Mary Poppins.* On television, Bill directed "The Mickey Mouse Club March," which opened each show. In 1965, Bill joined WED Enterprises to lend his talents to bringing to life the audio-animatronics figures in Great Moments with Mr. Lincoln, Mission to Mars, Pirates of the Caribbean, the Haunted Mansion, the Country Bear Jamboree, America Sings, and many others. Bill retired in 1979 and was named a Disney Legend in 1996.

I interviewed Bill on October 12, 1978, at WED, immediately after my interview with X Atencio. Bill's office was filled with cutout figures that served as models of potential theme park attractions. Bill was very generous with his time and his stories and I enjoyed seeing him at Disney-related events over the years.

DP: How did you happen to go to work for Disney?

BJ: My sister was kind of an artist. She's older than I am. I used to sit and draw or try to draw anything she was drawing. When I went to high school, I took four hours a day of art for four years. When I got out of high school, I got a scholarship to go to art school. So I went to art school for five years in Indianapolis. I hustled around trying to find a job after I finished. The best job I could find was painting show cards for a department store, "Sale $1.98" or something like that. So I wasn't too happy with that. I also had another job. I was working for an ice company, and I worked there full time. They got me a job with their advertising agency as a part-time artist. So I was working there when I ran across an ad in *Esquire* magazine that Disney needed artists to help finish up on *Snow White*.

DP: Do you remember what year?

BJ: 1937. So I wrote in, answered the ad. They sent out a questionnaire, and they had different problems and things that you were supposed to draw. Then you sent in your drawings and you'd hear from them. The funny thing was that there were three or four other artists in the advertising agency, and [when] I told them that I had done this, they said, "Oh, you'll never hear from them. We've done that." I thought, "Oh, well, I won't hear from them." A day or so later, I got a telegram. "A letter will follow," it said, "but please think about coming to California. We liked your samples." I came out here on a trial basis. For a month, we got $12.50 a week, and we were supposed to go through this schooling to see if they wanted us or if we liked the work or whatever. So there were thirty of us in the class from all over the country, and at the end of the month, they hired twelve of us.

DP: That must have been kind of a tense month.

BJ: Oh, it was rough. We went to school or you might call it a training class all day, and then we spent three hours at night drawing from models and stuff, and half a day Saturday.

DP: Was that with Don Graham?
BJ: Don Graham. Yeah.

DP: Was the daytime program with George Drake?
BJ: George Drake was there, but he didn't have much to do with it. The guy that really criticized our inbetweens and everything else was John Donne. It was in the old annex on Hyperion. That's one of the buildings that they moved out to the new studio. It used to be Publicity and I think Personnel is in there now.

DP: So when you came in, was this towards the latter part of *Snow White?*
BJ: The last six months of *Snow White.*

DP: That would have been an exciting time, I imagine.
BJ: Oh, yeah. They had a big premiere and everything! It was the biggest thing that ever happened to Walt and his people.

DP: Did you become an inbetweener?
BJ: As soon as we got out of the training class, we learned to inbetween. I worked I guess about five months doing inbetweens on *Snow White.*

DP: Who did you work with?
BJ: I worked first with Art Babbitt on the Wicked Queen. Then I got to do some inbetweens on some of the dwarfs. They were the ones that I really wanted to work on, because they were the cute ones. The Wicked Queen was just a bunch of little mouth movements when she was talking in the mirror. It wasn't too much fun to do.

DP: Did you work with Frank Thomas?
BJ: Later on, I worked with Frank and Ollie [Johnston] and Eric [Larson] when I worked on *Bambi.*

DP: That's right. They set up a special animation unit to work on that.

BJ: I worked with Woolie [Wolfgang Reitherman] for about two and a half years. I was first his inbetweener, and then I was his breakdown man, and then I became his assistant. Then he told me I was ready to animate, so from working with Woolie, I went into animation as an animator.

DP: You worked on "The Pastoral" in *Fantasia?*

BJ: Yeah.

DP: It looks like you worked on all the features right through the war: *Bambi, Saludos Amigos, Victory through Air Power.*

BJ: I had screen credit on twenty features and forty-seven short subjects as an animator.

DP: After the war, which sequence did you work on in *Make Mine Music?*

BJ: "All the Cats Join In." I did a lot of the jitterbug dancing and the piano keys and things like that. That was a good little picture then. At that time, instead of making a complete cartoon feature, they made things like *Make Mine Music.*

DP: Many historians see that as a period where these films were economically feasible when a feature wasn't. As Walt Disney said, after the war, they were kind of picking up the pieces, trying to get going again. But then some critics see these films as well below the level of the prewar and some of the postwar work. Did you feel—

BJ: I think some of these were pretty good, though. Like *Ben and Me* was a very good little short subject. "Pecos Bill" was pretty good.

DP: I grew up with "Johnny Appleseed" and those other films. Was there a feeling around the studio in that postwar period that it was a struggle to survive, to come out of that period and get on your feet again?

BJ: Well, we really weren't aware of that. The thing that really shook us up was the fact that years ago, when we were making short subjects— eighteen to twenty-four a year—there was a demand for them, because

the theatergoer would see a feature picture and a newsreel and a cartoon
short subject or a live-action short subject, like the Pete Smith Special-
ties. That was the bill. The theater owners really kind of paid extra, as I
understand it, for a Walt Disney short subject. Okay, so we had a good
market for that. But when they decided to have the double features
where they had two full-length live-action films, they didn't want any
newsreels or cartoons or anything, because they wanted to get that audience out of there and turn over another audience. So we were just practically forced out of the short-subject business. That was about 1953–54,
along in there, when that happened. I started directing in about 1954
until I came over here, which was 1965.

DP: In discussing the short subjects—Disney's contribution and the
contribution of other studios—one viewpoint among critics is that
while Disney led the short subjects throughout the 1930s, as the studio
turned to feature films and Walt Disney's personal attention turned to
feature films, some of the other studios came up with characters and
an approach that rivaled Disney. Some critics feel that they surpassed
Disney.

BJ: I always felt that we made the best product, whatever it was, but I
admired the different styles. For instance, I think there was some real
fine animation in the Tom and Jerry series. And then, of course, Mr.
Magoo and the things that were made at UPA were entirely different
than the kind of things we were doing, and they had a charm to them.
They had a different approach, really. Instead of trying to get natural
action and more realistic personalities into the characters, they had more
of a slapstick approach and what we might call limited animation that
we weren't allowed to do. We didn't approach that kind of thing at all. It
wasn't our bag. Then [John] Hubley made some pictures that were complete opposite of what Disney might do. I think some of the so-called
sophisticates thought that was the way to go. I just don't think they have
the charm. They don't have the heart to them, but I guess there is a market for all of them. One of my favorites was *The Country Cousin* [1936].
One of the most beautiful little cartoons you'd ever want to see. About
a year ago, when I was down at Disneyland, I went into the Fantasyland

Theater. There were three short subjects running in there from the 1930s. One of them was *The Band Concert* [1935], another was *Mickey's Trailer* [1938], and there was—

DP: *Thru the Mirror*, with the Fred Astaire style of dancing.

BJ: Yeah, *Thru the Mirror*. I sat in there and there were some young people—not just teenagers, but young adults in there—and they were just knocking themselves out. I thought, "God, these people haven't seen this stuff before!" This is one reason I was trying to get Mickey's Madhouse [a Disney parks attraction concept] going, and I think we still might do it.

DP: I hope so. It sounds like a great idea.

BJ: In contrast to Dumbo's Circus [another attraction concept], which would be all bright colors—gaudy circus colors—right next door to it we would feature Mickey's Madhouse in glorious black and white! It would be a ride-through. You'd see film clips of these old cartoons on each screen, there would be about five or six different scenes, and there'd be an overall music track. Fun music, with maybe Goofy playing a washboard here, and you'd hear the washboard sound, and maybe Mickey's on a bunch of pots and pans over there, and you would hear [the sound] from there. So as you go through, you'd see all these different things, and we'd have little animated figures, dimensional figures, that would keep time to the music, like [It's a] Small World.

DP: Or the Mickey Mouse Review [then at Walt Disney World].

BJ: Yeah. That would set the mood for this thing, and each time you'd go through there, you'd probably see a different scene on these screens, you see. Then in the second room, your car would start to climb up through an old dilapidated castle-looking thing. On the screens in there, there'd be ghosts and goblins and skeletons and black cats and torture chambers and all this weird stuff: lightning and thunder and screeches and screams and bats and all kind of spooky stuff. As you go through there, you climb, climb, climb, and then you get to the top of the building. When you break out of that, you come down through a thrill ride that takes you through train tunnels and through a tornado from *The Band Concert*. The car would just break loose and go fast. We'd have projected things going by you.

DP: That sounds great!

BJ: I think it would be a wonderful ride. It would bring back memories to those people that had seen some of that stuff, and it'd be a whole new experience to the younger generation.

DP: I think they would love it.

BJ: It would be a different ride. I think it would be real popular. What I'd like to do out front [is use] the logo that used to come on the screen years ago. This was before your time. When a black and white Mickey Mouse cartoon came on the screen, the whole audience would scream, just like they do for Elvis or Frank Sinatra or somebody like that! That's what I wanted to have on the facade of the building. A great big head of Mickey Mouse, so that you'd see this thing from a block away, and I bet you kids would start running.

DP: What were your first impressions of Walt Disney?

BJ: I was there, I guess, about twelve or thirteen years before I was ever even in a meeting with him, because the animation directors and the story men would be in the meetings with him. Once in a while, the animators would be in a sweatbox with him where he was looking at a picture, but then they would have a meeting afterward and discuss what was wrong with the picture or how they could improve it, but the animators really weren't included very much in meetings with Walt. So although I worked there twelve or thirteen years, I really didn't know him at all until after I became a director, where I was more closely involved and was in many meetings with him. I got to the point where I wasn't afraid to talk to him!

DP: When you did start to work with him, how did you find him to be?

BJ: When I was first included in meetings, I wouldn't say anything. I'd just sit there and listen to what he had to say and whatever they were

discussing. And then finally one day, he turned to me and he said, "What
do you think, Bill?" I told him what I thought, and I guess he liked it,
because from then on, he would give me that funny look like, "Okay, let's
hear it." And I would talk. But it was strange. There were a lot of people
that had to go to those meetings, and they would echo everything that
he said, and he would really be rude to them, because he didn't want to
hear what they had to say.

DP: He didn't want yes-men, in other words.
BJ: No. He'd cut that off; right as soon as they'd start to talk, he'd start
talking. Everybody would listen to him; they'd just shut up.

DP: The fingers would start tapping . . .
BJ: Yeah, and coughing.

DP: So your connection with him was more of a positive one than I guess
some people had.
BJ: I think he appreciated what I was trying to do, and he was wonderful
to me, I mean, financially and every other way, and seemed to appreciate
what I did, although he never came out and said it!

DP: Well, I guess the fact that you remained over the years is a way of
complimenting you. When you were working on the cutout figures, I
gather that he was kind of intrigued with doing that kind of thing.
BJ: I really know why, too, because what happened was that animation was getting so expensive, the short subjects that had a budget of
say $40,000–$60,000 around the early 1950s were running $125,000–
$200,000, and it was just getting to the point where it was almost
impractical to make them because of salaries and everything else. They
called me in one time in a meeting and said, "Bill, we want you to
think about something." I said, "What?" They said, "How can we make
entertainment cheaper, Disney-quality film cheaper?" So I thought,
"Gee, that's quite a problem!" I woke up in the middle of the night and
I thought, "If I could make cute little things out of Necco wafers and
cutouts and attach them with flexible things like rubber bands or chains

or things and move them [in] stop-motion, I might be able to make them fairly cheap. If I had a good story, maybe they'd be entertaining." So I went in the following Monday morning and I told X [Atencio]. X was working with me at that time. I told him what I had in mind. He said, "Yeah, it sounds crazy. Let's try it." So we went to the hobby shop and we spent about $4 or $5 and went back and started designing little things. We only spent a day or two monkeying around. We made some rabbits and some little Indians and several little characters. I called Dick Drills over in Camera, and I said, "I want to shoot some stuff, and I'm going to bring my backgrounds and I'm just going to move things one frame at a time or two frames at a time and see what I can do." So he said okay. I went over the next day and I worked about half a day and I shot seventy-five feet of film, stop-motion. It didn't have any story to it or anything. It was just a bunch of crazy stuff, just to see how it would move. And it moved. I don't know whatever became of the film. I hope it's in the archives. But anyway, I showed it to Walt. He was fascinated with it and interested in it, and he asked me why I did it. I told him that Harry Tytle and some of the guys had asked me to think about something [that could be made cheaper], and this was my answer. He said, "Well, let's get a story going." That's when we got into stop-motion. The first stop-motion were the titles for *The Shaggy Dog*. We made that dog out of an old shaggy mop and it had eyeballs in it and a tongue, and it chased a butterfly and all that. That was the first actual production that I did with stop-motion.

DP: Was *Jack and Old Mac* stop-motion?

BJ: No, that was just real simplified animation. That was the first thing I did really because of this thing they wanted, to do something cheaper. *The Shaggy Dog* thing was kind of funny. I shot all those titles. It took me a week to do it under the camera, because I'd animate the dog coming in and maybe sniffing something, and then we'd change the names behind him. He was big enough so that he would cover the credit and then at a certain point, I'd change the names that he was covering up. Then as he'd move out, he'd leave the new names there. That was the principle of the whole thing. Oh, I worked like a slave doing those things and trying to get the most out of that dumb dog that I could, as much personality as I knew how to put into it as an animator. It came out pretty nice. I showed it to Walt, and he was real pleased with it. The following day, Bob Jabow, who was head of Camera, called me and said, "We can't use that film [for] *The Shaggy Dog* titles." I said, "What? I just showed it to Walt yesterday, and he liked it." He said, "Well, it's not of good enough quality. It's all underexposed. If we tried to show it in a drive-in, you wouldn't be able to see it." I said, "Well, what can we do about it?" He said, "It'll have to be shot over." I said, "The deadline's already passed. They didn't even call me to do it until it was really too late." He said, "Well, we can't use it. You want me to tell Walt, or are you going to tell him?" I said, "It's my baby, I'll tell him." So I called Dolores [Voght, Disney's secretary] and said, "I've got to see Walt." She said, "Not today you don't." I said, "What do you mean?" She said, "He's shooting live-action lead-ins. I understand he doesn't like the dialogue that was written for him, and he's having a hell of a time with it. He's not in a very good mood." I said, "Well, I can't help it. I've got to see him anyway." So I went over there, and I stood and watched him until he got through a take that he was having trouble with.

DP: This was for the TV show?

BJ: The TV show lead-in where he was at his desk and talking. So finally he made a good take, and he sat down. He looked over at me, and he said, "What are you doing here?" I said, "I've got to talk to you." He said, "Okay, what is it?" I told him that Bob Jabow had called me and said the titles weren't good enough. He said, "Can you shoot them over?" I said, "Yes, I can shoot them over, and I think I can do a better job now that I've seen them." He said, "Well, fine. How long will it take you?" I said, "It took me a week before. I think I can do it in maybe three days." He said, "The deadline's pretty close." I started to walk away, and he said, "Bill? By the way, when you redo them, put your names on the credits." X and I and T[hornton]. Hee. So it wasn't such a bad day after all!

DP: Catch him in a bad mood more often!

BJ: We had some fun when we did credits for *Bon Voyage*. We popped champagne bottles, and we had escargot on the set where we show this beautiful table setup. We did a lot of crazy things on that one. We also did *The Parent Trap*. That had kind of interesting titles. We made some little dolls that were supposed to be like Hayley Mills and her sister. They were kind of interwoven into the titles. The titles were all to a song. We also did—

DP: *Babes in Toyland?*
BJ: I never worked so hard in my life as I did on *Babes in Toyland*. All that stop-motion stuff. In some scenes, I had as many as forty soldiers marching and each soldier had twelve pairs of legs that had to be changed every two frames.

DP: Sounds tedious.
BJ: Oh, God! It would take me about fifteen minutes to change their legs, and to be sure, I'd have to put a magnet down. They had magnetic feet so they wouldn't fall over. The ground or the table they were performing on had a metal top covered with background paper in whatever color we were supposed to have. Then the magnet would hold the soldier up. I'd put the magnet behind his feet so his foot wouldn't slide, to mark him, and then put him back down in the same spot with his different legs. You'd change four in a row, four in the next row, and you'd have ten or twelve rows of those guys. It was tedious work. I'd have to move their arms just so, each frame, just like animation, only it was all up here.

DP: I guess you'd have to have a good sense of timing.
BJ: Well, twelve pairs of legs meant that he was marching in twelve tempo, so that the rhythm was always there. That way, it's easy to divide it down into musical beats. If music is on elevens or sevens or something like that, it just doesn't divide into twenty-four, and that's the reason. A lot of times in animation, you're animating to music, so that you have a beat on your exposure sheet every so many frames, and you make everything happen on those beats so those musical accents will stand out. If you're not animating to music, then the musician will write to your action that you have in your animation. But most of the things that I was involved in, except for the chipmunks [Chip 'n Dale], involved

music. For those special titles, they had to write a title song. For *Babes in Toyland*, there was "The March of the Toys." All those things had a definite beat to them. We had to pay very close attention to that.

DP: I guess if you got off tempo, it would be obvious as soon as you looked at it. I have a couple of old home-movie prints of some early Disney films, including *The Klondike Kid* (1932), and they are silent, but you can see the rhythm because Mickey Mouse is moving to the beat. I can imagine what the music sounds like. In my classes, everybody loves the black and white cartoons with the vintage Mickey Mouse.

BJ: When I was working on Mickey's Madhouse, which I worked on for four or five months, I looked at one hundred old black and white short subjects that were made from 1928 until 1934. Along about 1934 is when they started getting into color. I wanted these to be the old authentic black and whites, and I chose certain footage from the different pictures that I wanted to use. Like in the musical part of the thing that I told you about, in the first big room that you go through, everything would have to do with music. They'd either be playing instruments or dancing, that kind of thing. Then in the next room with the spooky stuff, I chose a lot of stuff like *The Skeleton Dance* and *Lonesome Ghosts* and a bunch of funny things. Those old black and white cartoons had a lot of nutty stuff that nobody would ever do now. They had a lot of spitting gags and they had a lot of panty gags. The drop seat would fall open someway!

DP: All the scenes with the cows' udders!

BJ: Cows' udders! I had that in Mickey's Madhouse.

DP: Well, it's certainly obvious that the audience sophistication changed over the years. But then maybe that's part of the appeal. Mickey became such a straight character that maybe part of the appeal of the old Mickey is that he's a little more adventurous and a little more worldly.

BJ: He was funny in those days. Then he got to be like a good little Boy Scout. The story men just had trouble with him because of his personality.

DP: Do you think that there is any truth to the idea that Mickey Mouse was Walt Disney's alter ego and that as Walt evolved over the years from a young producer in a struggling studio to eventually becoming a television host, Mickey kind of followed suit?

BJ: I don't see any relation at all. One thing that kind of upsets me is that they are celebrating Mickey's fiftieth anniversary. I don't think the kids want to relate to a fifty-year-old mouse. They don't want to relate to anybody that's fifty years or older. They want people of their own generation. All of their idols are young people. To me, it's a shame to think of Mickey as being fifty years old.

DP: I guess I don't think of him as being fifty years old, because he doesn't look older. The beauty of Mickey is that he is intangible; you can't touch him as you can the Mickey at Disneyland. It's like a Santa Claus in a department store versus your image of Santa Claus when you're a little kid. They are much more fun when not put into real terms.

BJ: Right.

DP: I am interested in the studio strike. I was wondering how you fit in with that. Were you a striker? A nonstriker?

BJ: Well, at that time, I was so interested in animation that the night before the strike happened was the first time I had heard anything about it. I know a lot of guys had been having meetings and talking about it and all that, and boy, this came as a complete surprise to me. I went to a meeting and I heard all this strike talk and everything, how everybody hated everybody else, and how nobody made any money, and all this stuff, and they were going to close down the studio. Jeez! I was dumbfounded, you know! I thought, "This is not for me. I'm going to get out of here." So I just got out. The next morning, I went to work. I didn't want to hear any more of that stuff.

DP: Did you have any problems going through the—

BJ: Oh, yeah. They scratched my car up and tried to turn it over one time.

DP: Really!

BJ: Called you all kinds of names. People that you knew and that you had worked with. They were on the other side, and you were on your own side. At that time, I had been animating for maybe a year, maybe not quite a year. When they made the settlement of the strike, [that was] the only time I ever got set back. One of the deals was that they would have so many animators, so many directors, so many people who would be hired back, and so many stayed. They guaranteed me that I would go back to animation after ninety days. I guess it was a union punishment to be put down because you had been working or something. Like Ham Luske, who had been a director for several years, he had to go back to being an animator. So I worked with Ham Luske for three months. At the end of the three months, I went back to animation. That was the strike, and there were a lot of bitter feelings that never were healed.

DP: Yeah, they're still there, I think, with some people. Did you find it hard to work with some of the strikers after it was settled?

BJ: Well, when people call you names, you know, it's hard to forget. I know that there were feelings that never were healed in a lot of cases. Then there were other people that were really looking for the good in all of us, I guess, that came out of it all right.

DP: Did the tension that existed after the strike tend to dissipate at all when Art Babbitt left?

BJ: That helped. I know he had a bad time, because he'd walk down the hall and people would just turn their head. He was treated terribly. In fact, I know he was very uncomfortable even being there.

DP: In some accounts, he seems to be the focal point of the strikers.

BJ: Yeah. He was kind of the rabble-rouser that got them all stirred up. I know a lot of artists, a lot of good artists really couldn't—you see, the Disney product was always a result of a lot of teamwork. You might have been a real good artist, but you had your own way of working, you wanted to express your own personality that didn't go along with what was being done. For instance, the background painters are a lot of terrific artists, and a lot of them are great landscape painters who sell a lot of their own work. Well, when they're painting for a picture, the backgrounds have to look pretty much alike through a certain sequence and then lead into the next sequence. There has to be a transition of mood and color and so forth that is coordinated through the making of a feature picture where they work as a team. A lot of artists just couldn't bring themselves to be on the team. They were too independent, and some of them weren't capable. You know, I don't mean that they're all terrific artists, that they're just too stubborn to do the work, but a lot of them weren't capable of it. A lot of the guys in animation, they had so much talent, but they weren't talented enough to be an animator. They would bitch, bitch, bitch, bitch, you know. Once they had the opportunity to do it, they found out they couldn't do it. They weren't good enough to be Disney animators. You get so much flak and so much criticism and so much downgrading of Disney and the Disney Studio and the Disney product and everything from a lot of these people that either didn't want to do it or didn't like the way it was done or weren't able to help. A lot of your key people in other studios that were very successful were Disney people.

DP: That's what it seems like. I guess the core artists at UPA were former Disney people. Can you tell me about your transition to WED?

BJ: Walt sent me over here to help on the audio-animatronics animation because of my knowledge of animation. They needed somebody here that was a trained animator, that could interpret animation into these figures. I've always felt that things like America Sings and the Pirates [of the Caribbean] and things like that are fun to do, because you're doing a cartoon-type of thing, whereas [Great Moments with] Mr. Lincoln is the hardest thing in the world to do. I don't think that the state of the art is good enough to do something like that. It comes off fairly well, but I know myself that I have never been satisfied. I've programmed the one that's in [Walt] Disney World. I programmed both Washington and Lincoln, and I've never been proud of their performance because they are so limited. For instance, standing up and sitting down. An ordinary person—I always think in terms of footage—it takes about three feet to stand up from a sitting position, and it takes two and a half feet to sit down. Well, if I tried real hard to get him to stand up in those time limits, when he'd hit the top, he'd just vibrate. When you sit or stand up slowly, watch what happens [demonstrates].

DP: That looks like Mr. Lincoln.

BJ: That's about the speed he goes. It looks like he's got a bad back, and it always will look that way, because I can make him go faster, and I can make him sit down faster, but he'll vibrate at the top—he'll tear himself up—and if he sits down faster, he'll break the chair. So what choice do you have?

DP: I understand. I guess most people don't realize how much power is involved in those figures.

BJ: Oh, God! If he raised his arm up, and you were standing there, he'd lift you right off the stage. He could lift five hundred pounds just by doing that.

DP: One thing I noticed at the Hall of Presidents and with Lincoln at Disneyland that I think is really effective is the movement when they are just sitting there while the narrator is talking, the head turning looking at the audience. At the Hall of Presidents, I could see the light reflect off of Harry Truman's glasses as he turned his head.

BJ: That's one of the reasons I was asked to program, just that particular problem. You have to be a movie director and an animator to appreciate what is supposed to happen. The audience is supposed to watch Lincoln and listen to him talk, but for the other figures, it's just like a crowd scene. The other figures still have to be alive, but there's no scratching or combing their hair or blowing their nose or anything like that that could steal the scene, so it's a very subtle thing to make them move just enough to keep alive, but not to steal the scene. But you watch each one of them, like two of them kind of chat together, and they look, and they nod at each other, and they agree with Lincoln here and there, and there are eye blinks and they change their weight from one foot to another, or they might move their head a little bit. Just enough to keep them alive and not to attract your attention.

DP: It's really effective.

BJ: It's a subtle problem really with a stage that big. Wathel Rogers and I are the only two that do any programming. The way I approach these things, first we get the mouth working properly. Ken O'Brien does most of that before I get the figure. Then I listen to the dialogue, and I know that the first thing I try is to get his head turned to look in the right way. [In the Country Bear Jamboree,] he looks over here at Gomer, he looks over that way at Wendell, he looks up that way at Teddi Barra in the swing. So the first thing after the mouth movement, I run the knob with the head turns, and I get him looking from one place to another. Then the next thing is the head nods, so that when he says "I" and he's looking up at Teddi Barra, I have his head tilted higher or nod his head higher. Then when you turn your head from side to side, when you look to the right, your head usually tilts slightly that way. So as soon as I get through with all those three deals, then I've got him looking in the right direction, and he begins to come to life. Then after that, I do eye blinks and eye turns. When you are attracted to something over here, the first thing that moves are your eyes, then your head follows, and you usually blink before and after the turn.

DP: That's amazing that you are aware of all of that!

BJ: So you put all of this information into that bear head and pretty soon, he looks like he's thinking and talking and looking around! And hell, he's just a stuffed bear! Then after that, you get his body turns that work with the rest of it. Maybe he leans forward or maybe he leans back when he looks up there. All of these things kind of loosen him up. Then, if he's got a guitar, he looks down at the guitar, and he's got the rhythm going with this hand. When you turn this knob in tempo with the music, he responds just like that—sometimes not as fast as I would like it. But anyway, then you get the hand slide going up and down. No musician is ever going to think that he's playing the chords, but it looks pretty good. You accumulate all these things and you run it with the music and the dialogue, and pretty soon, the bear begins to come to life. Marc Davis and Al Bertino planned the whole show, wrote the dialogue, designed the characters, and all this stuff. Then Blaine Gibson and his crew sculpted them.

Then they get cast over at MAPO [the manufacturing arm of WED, incorporated in 1965 and named after Mary Poppins], and then other people put the fur cloth on them and do the makeup and the costuming. Then they come over here and they set them up and hook them up to this machine, and I get to make them come to life! This is the fun part of it.

DP: It's amazing, because everything you say is true, but it's not the kind of thing—unless, I guess, you were animating—that you might be aware of.

BJ: I can tell you a true story that I heard from Freddy Moore. Freddy was one of the best animators years ago, and his drawings were just fantastic. He was the one that kind of put cuteness into the Disney product with the dwarfs, the Three Little Pigs, and stuff like that. But Freddy told me—and he told other people, too—that one morning Walt came into his room and he was real excited. He said, "Say, Freddy, do you know when you blink your eyes, the lower lid doesn't move?" So when you're thinking about animation, the tiniest little thing in analyzing good animation is important. This is the kind of thinking that a Disney animator does that a lot of other people wouldn't even consider.

DP: But that is probably the thing that has made the Disney animation the best, that attention to detail.

BJ: That's right.

DP: Sometimes when I think of all the work that went into something like *Pinocchio* or *Snow White*, I wonder how many of the people that see the film have any idea of the work that went into it. The average person can't sit there and appreciate all this unless they know about it. But it is their experience of the film, I guess, where it all pays off.

BJ: I think that it has been proven that people appreciate it, because those films will still go out and make money again and again and again. People that have seen them before like to see them again, and people that haven't seen them are delighted to see them for the first time. The film library over there will last forever, I hope.

Lou Debney

Lou Debney was born on January 3, 1916. He and Les Clark, one of the Nine Old Men of Animation, knew each other and Walt and Roy Disney from the Kingswell Avenue studio neighborhood before Lou and Les came to work for the studio. Lou joined Disney two weeks after his eighteenth birthday, working first in the Cutting Department at the Hyperion Studio and then becoming an assistant director on *Snow White* with Ben Sharpsteen. Lou worked as an assistant to a number of directors on both features and short subjects. After work on the live-action film *Perri* (1957), Lou became a producer on *The Mickey Mouse Club* and *Zorro*. He later became a production coordinator on the Disney television anthology series, a position he still held when I interviewed him at the studio on July 18, 1980.

Lou was very friendly and peppered his stories with a healthy dose of profanity, which may or may not survive the editor's delete button. He was the last person to participate in my first round of interviews. He died on April 8, 1986. Everyone talks about Walt's ability to find talent and to develop it to meet his needs. Lou, Les Clark, and Ruthie Tompson all had successful careers at Disney and all came out of the first studio neighborhood. While Walt gathered artists from all over the world, many of his best people were home grown.

DP: I understand that you used to sell newspapers to Walt and Roy Disney.
LD: Yes, this was before the Hyperion studio. I sold papers on Kingswell [Avenue] and Vermont [Avenue], and Roy and Walt had their first studio before Hyperion maybe 150 feet off Vermont. There are pictures downstairs [in the Animation Building] of the Kingswell studio.

DP: Yes, I've driven down that street.
LD: Oh, well, then you know it. I was right there on the corner. Yes, I got to know them well. I wasn't particularly interested in animated cartoons at that particular phase of my life. They always called me Whitey until the very end. I guess there might be one or two that still call me Whitey, which is all right. I never cared. What the hell! Yes, I did sell papers to both of them. As a matter of fact, while I was still selling papers, young Roy [Roy Edward Disney] was born to Roy and Edna, and Roy used to hold young Roy in his arms on my corner, talking to me while his wife was in the market shopping. We always had a great rapport. Roy was, of course, easier, quite a different personality, as you've heard by now, than Walt's, although Walt was just super to me—just super to me. But Roy, through the years I've known his boy growing up and then working with him in later years, and then his children I've gotten to know, and God, it seems like I'm an old man, but I'm really not! I love to ski and I'm active.

DP: Well, if you were selling papers, you had to be pretty young.
LD: Yes, I guess I was eleven or twelve in those days. Get this! I'm on the corner selling papers. If I would get a dollar and I had just started the afternoon's work, I'd have to go onto this little beanery, Mr. Ferris's little restaurant, and get change from Les Clark. Before Les started work-ing for Walt, I knew Les. And then in later years, when I started at the studio, I took out his sister. I've known the father [James Clark, studio security guard] and the mother [Lute, homemaker] and Mickey Clark

[Disney studio employee later with Retlaw (*Walter* spelled backward), Walt's personal company].

DP: Did knowing Walt and Roy lead to your going to work for them?

LD: Well, now to jump ahead a little bit, Don, I used to go up to Santa Barbara. I had a girlfriend there, and [we'd] go to the theater. One night, I saw *Lullaby Land* (1933), the old Silly Symphony. It was then I got the adrenalin shock of, "My God, this is sheer magic!" The sheer magic of it turned me on. I was only a half-assed cartoonist like many kids are in junior high school and high school, but I felt closer to Roy, and I wrote to let him know that I'm his old friend, Whitey, and I'd like to be considered to do some work at the studio on Hyperion. I lived, oh, probably a fifteen-minute walk [from the studio], and John Marshall High School, where I went, was only a block up the street. It was just before Christmas, and his secretary wrote back that Roy was in New York, "but you can be sure, Mr. Debney, that your letter will be brought to his attention the minute he gets back." I turned eighteen on January 3, and within two weeks after that, he wrote me a letter and had me come over. He introduced me to Bill Garrity, who was the head of the whole operation, not on the creative side, but on projection, recording, editing, camera, and that phase. I was mechanically inclined; that would sum up why I thought I might fit in. They did hire me for $12.50 a week. I started in the Cutting Department, assembling pencil tests. At that time, there was Bob Cook, who later became head of the Sound Department and Editorial Department, and one other man, Jim Loury. Jim came out from Kansas City. Sam Slyfield was really the head of Sound then and Bob took over the Cutting [Department]. And that's how it started there.

This is my first [job]. I would cut the film, assemble it, put the dialogue with it or the sound effects, thread the machine. The first sweatbox was not as big as this room. Jaxon [director Wilfred Jackson] is sitting on the floor with a cigar. I'd roll [the film], and they'd back up, and they'd analyze the scene a little more, take another second here, eight frames there. Then they might say, "Whitey, could you try this cut?" I'd pull those things out, run to the cutting [equipment], zip, zip, splice it together—while they were sitting there—put it back on, and run it.

Now, they could see it instantly. Today, you have a screening, and next Tuesday, you might [see the changes]. The whole goddamn enthusiasm seems to have dissipated, but Jaxon, with that cigar in the projection room, sitting there all the time!

DP: Did it seem strange to have known them as a newsboy and then to be working there?

LD: No, it didn't seem strange, because it was my neighborhood. I didn't come out from the East or from the North; this is where I went to school, up the street. I dropped out of high school and came to work in January 1934. Walt and Roy lived almost across the street from the high school on Lyric [Street]. I'd pass their houses when I'd go home. Sometimes Walt would be out; sometimes Roy would be out. I was on my home territory, so it didn't seem strange. It took a short while to make me fully realize what a coup this was to find this house of magic so close by. I had many of my friends still going to John Marshall and then graduating and going on to UCLA or [the University of Southern California] or different places. I kept all my friendships there. It was interesting the number of people that said, "Gee, Debney's over there. Why don't I drop in there?" So we got Erwin Verity and then later, Card Walker and Carl Nader, Bob Jabow and Art Jabow, and a number of guys. They started in Traffic. But no, it was always super, particularly when we got on the bonus plan, and I would bring home a bonus check or show Card Walker a bonus check of 150 bucks on *Snow White*, let's say. Card graduated from UCLA in the spring, I guess, of 1938. He had been a very good friend of mine and lived in the neighborhood. I'm going off on a little different tangent here, but it was a case of, "Well, now I've graduated. What the hell am I going to do?" His dad was with Arden Dairy in promotion/sales, and he had spent summers working in the sales end of Arden Dairy Ice Cream. I said, "I happen to have a very fine friend at the studio, a wise man, Mr. Gunther Lessing," who was our first legal eagle. He had a son the same age as me. Gunther just treated me like a son. It was easy for me to say, "Mr. Lessing, I've got a very good friend of mine I'd like you to spend a few minutes with and see what you can line up." "Oh, sure." So I brought Card in and introduced them and left. That afternoon, I found out that he was going to start the following Monday in the Camera Department. [Card Walker went on to become the president of the Walt Disney Company in 1971.] To this day, we are still very close friends. By sheer coincidence, Card has a son who is about twenty-two. I have a son who is twenty-four. My son's name is John Cardon Debney [a Disney composer], and his son's name is John Cardon Walker. The two are best of friends.

I stayed with the Cutting Department. The Camera Department was right downstairs, and we got to know the whole operation. It was then, while we were getting started on the preliminary story sketches and everything, shooting what we used to call Leica reels on *Snow White*, that I was set up to be the man that would assemble all the tests from all the sequences in *Snow White*. I guess it was in a matter of months that Ben Sharpsteen was assigned as a sequence director on the film. Ben and I always got along real great. Ben wanted me to switch from the Cutting Department to assistant direction, which was a very easy transition to make. While I was with Ben, we finished *Two-Gun Mickey* (1934), the last black and white cartoon. We were together for many, many shorts. I guess maybe one of the things that attracted Ben to me—I like to think one of the things—was sort of a flair that I had for sound effects. I found it just a great unexplored area really, to get involved with sound effects. They really gave me carte blanche to record sound effects [in house] or go off the lot. I remember when we were doing *Snow White* and the [scene where the] witch pries the rock, and she falls and it falls, I went over to Columbia and I bought some sound effects for a buck a foot or something, maybe forty dollars worth of thunder and lightning from, I guess it was, the old Frank Capra movie *Lost Horizon*. The animators, when they would bring me their tests to be assembled in continuity, and they wanted them to be enhanced, it was fun finding sound effects. Woolie [Wolfgang Reitherman] would do the Goof on a surfboard and he would crash, and we would get snare drums rolling and cymbals, bong. So I helped a lot of scenes get over by adding sound effects, and many were retained.

Then, after my sessions with Ben Sharpsteen, which seemed like a number of years, Walt wanted to make a director out of Jack Kinney on

Pinocchio. So he moved me over with Jack, and I tried to take over everything in the music room, leaving strictly creative functions to Jack Kinney and Ralph Wright. They would develop stories and I would be there
when they recorded, handling all the recordings, the assembly of tracks,
the making of exposure sheets. I worked with Jack for a long time. We
did many in the "How to" series. Then after that, I remember on *Pinocchio*,
Walt wanted to make a director out of T[hornton]. Hee, so I moved over
and performed the same function [since he was] a new man, not familiar
with the routine. T and I worked together on many sequences on *Pinocchio*. Then I switched up and doubled up with Jaxon on certain sequences
on *Pinocchio*, including the sequence with Stromboli and the marionette
show. He was a sensitive man. He sort of wore blinders. I mean, he knew
what he was looking for. Jaxon was always a true sweetheart. He might say
in a low tone, "Whitey, when Pinocchio comes dancing down the steps, I
want it to have a little bit of character, instead of just jingling wood." He
knew what he wanted. In contrast, let's say, to Gerry Geronimi, who was a
"Goddammit, Whitey, it was better before you changed it!"

I guess at that time I was also involved with Jimmy Algar. I was his
assistant on "The Sorcerer's Apprentice" in *Fantasia* and then *Bambi*.
Then I switched over to Gerry Geronimi and we worked on *Susie, [the
Little] Blue Coupe* (1952), and then I worked on *Lady and the Tramp* and
Peter Pan. In about 1952 or 1953, I guess, I switched over to live action.
Walt then wanted to do his first True-Life Fantasy where we could do
more. We could use the word *fantasy* and get away with dream sequences
and so forth. Did you ever see *Perri*?

DP: Yes.

LD: Paul [Kenworthy] and I formed a team and went up to Utah and
Wyoming and Idaho, where we were thirty months together making
Perri. After *Perri*, I came back and got involved with the second year
of *The Mickey Mouse Club*. I was Bill Walsh's associate on a hundred
episodes. I had all the Mouseketeer sequences. I had fifteen minutes to
fill every day for twenty weeks. It was exciting to have a big storyboard.
Twenty weeks, five days a week, every day, blanks and then filling in
with names and story ideas that were fed to Bill Walsh and to me and

to Walt. Then after that, I switched over to associate producer with Bill Anderson. I think we did eighty-two shows of *Zorro*, where I was his production coordinator.

Then one day, Walt—you know, after twenty years—called me in, and he said, "Whitey, I think I've got something here that is going to make you." He gave me a script that Ellis Marcus had written, *Moochie of the Little League* (1959). Walt said, "I want you to read it, and I've got a couple of ideas, and you're going to produce these. I've got a couple of hundred thousand dollars for each episode." It was truly exciting. It starred little Kevin Corcoran playing Moochie.

DP: Yeah, I remember watching.

LD: I had to go out and see the teams. We wanted to use kids that could play ball—not Hollywood kids, although we had a few Hollywood kids like Kevin play on each team. But it was truly exciting. As a matter of fact, at that time on that picture, Ron Miller came to the studio and became the second assistant on the show. It was pretty damn thrilling, I have to say, to go one-on-one with Walt. We finally finished the two shows. Walt was interested in knowing how the expenses were going. I kept track of every last little detail. They came in for like $198,000 average per episode. I thought, "I'll drop off this information for Walt with his secretary." I said, "I think Walt will be interested in these numbers, Dolores [Voght, Disney's secretary]." So I was slipping out, and unbeknownst to me, he was right around the corner listening to me. "Hey, Whitey, you're sure you've got all the costs in there? I want everything in there, Technicolor's rights and all that." "Yeah, Walt, it's all in. This is it. The account is closed. You said I had $200,000 each. Fine." "Oh, good. Okay, Whitey. See you later." So I left. That evening, I dropped by Card's office. He was head of advertising, I guess. I said, "Let's go out." We were just getting to the little time gate when Walt's backing up his Packard convertible, and he swings around and gives us the high sign. I said, "He doesn't want to see me." So Card starts running over there, and Walt says, "No, no. Whitey! Whitey!" He said, "I just thought you'd like to know I put through a little raise for you." I said, "Oh, thanks, Walt." I've got to say it was a thrilling moment, you know.

Then after that, I was the assistant to the producer—Walt says, "I'm the producer"—on *Babes in Toyland*. "Goddammit," he says, "I don't know who in hell to get to play Mary in this thing." I said, "Well, Walt, in my opinion, if Columbia or Universal were making this, they'd probably be calling you, saying, 'Can we borrow Annette [Funicello]?'" She was very hot. Well, it turned out we got Annette and Tommy Sands. Walt thought Ray Bolger would be great for Barnaby. He said, "I remember Ray Bolger when I was taking a trip to Hawaii on a boat. Ray Bolger was there, and after dinner, why, he would perform. God, that guy can dance." "Fine, fine. If you like him, I like him." And then out of the *Zorro* series, we got Henry Calvin and Gene Sheldon. When it came to the director, it looked like Ward [Kimball] was going to direct it. He had been developing some sequences, and he shot some tests. But Walt just didn't think Ward would be right for it. Then Sidney Miller, because he had been directing the Mousketeers, his plea was, "I was born to direct *Babes in Toyland*. I played in it as an actor years ago. It's destiny that I direct it." Well, it turned out that Walt didn't think it was destiny that he direct it. But Jack Donahue, who had done a lot of Lucille Ball things, was an old hoofer and a director. Now, I'm giving you a little bit of insight on this particular production. We called in Art Vitarelli, who usually did stunts. He would do the rigging where people worked on wires. He would direct the second unit scenes. Art just felt strongly that it should be a director that had a musical background. Walt finally said, "All right, we'll get Jack Donahue." Now, Jack was a nice guy, just a great guy. But doggone it, he shot that damn show like he was shooting a stage presentation instead of a motion picture. There were damn few over-the-shoulder shots. We made a few bucks on it, but it never turned out to be the classic that we could bring out every year. So I don't have any claim to fame outside of the features I was involved in as a low peon on *Snow White* and *Bambi* and those things. I guess there might be six to eight features and a couple of dozen hour television shows I was an associate producer on, but nothing truly significant.

DP: When you were talking about *The Mickey Mouse Club*, that was interesting to me because I grew up with it. My brother was four years older, so we were in the right age group. We had such a strong attraction for the show that we used to kiss the TV set when Annette was on!

LD: Well, it was not unique. Out of all the kids, Darlene [Gillespie] was the most talented one for singing. Doreen [Tracey] was pretty good and then there was another little one that was the best dancer [Sharon Baird]. And Bobby [Burgess] was good. Cubby [O'Brien] was on the drums. Annette was cute. She'd had a little ballet, you know, couldn't sing too well, but you were not unusual. Her fan mail was twenty to one over all the rest. They wanted pictures, they wanted autographs, they wanted everything Annette. She certainly was not the most talented in the group, but she had that charisma that you have to have.

During the war—and this was one of the highlights of my life here—I was assigned to direct and had a great little unit here, a unit that was set up here to furnish animated editorial cartoons, for want of another nomenclature, for Frank Capra and the *Why We Fight* series. During meetings, I admit I was rather impressed by John Huston in uniform and Tony Veiller and Eric Knight and James Hilton—many big names that he had in his unit, which was established over on Western and Sunset Boulevard at the Fox [Studio on] Western Avenue. In a meeting with Walt and Frank Capra and some of his entourage and some of our boys, Walt set me up as the director for whatever Frank wanted. Interesting little story here. There must have been four or five from the studio, including myself, and Frank and Eric Knight. Eric Knight—they could have said Joe Schmo, [the name] meant nothing to me. It meant nothing to Walt. We broke for lunch and Walt goes his way, and Frank went his way. I ended up going [with a group] to the Blue Evening up in Toluca Lake. There was a secretary, Eric Knight, and a couple of others. I am a little bit uncomfortable, but I'm trying to relax. I'm representing Walt. It's all sort of new, this war business. Eric Knight was quite a dashing, sandy-haired character and very humorous. The woman said, "What do you think Eric was before he came to Hollywood?" I said, "Well, I'm sure he was an actor." She chuckled, and Eric chuckled, and she said, "No, Whitey, he is a writer. He wrote *This Above All*, *Lassie Come Home*, and *The Flying Yorkshireman*." I said, "Well, gee, that's great." I was vaguely familiar with a couple of them. We go back

to the studio and pick up where we left off. They are talking about a lot
of live action; we're not going to have anything to do with that. Walt
said, "Well, Frank, you're going to get a writer in on this and come with
a script, so we know exactly—" And Eric Knight said, "Please, Mr. Disney, I'm going to be the writer." Walt just looked and said, "Okay. Fine."
So that was my cue to take my pen out and write, "Walt, Eric Knight
wrote *Lassie Come Home* and *The Flying Yorkshireman*," and I just folded
it up and while these guys are talking handed it to Walt. "Well, for
Christ sake, why didn't somebody tell me?" He goes up to Eric Knight
and shakes hands with him. And from then on, Eric went to lunch with
Walt! He and Walt became great friends. He was Walt's kind of guy.

In the early part of the war years, at one of those meetings with
Frank Capra, Frank said, "Walt, a couple of questions: How much is this
going to cost, and when am I going to get it?" Walt's very simple answer,
which I've repeated many times, "Well, Frank, there are nickel cigars and
dollar cigars. We can give it to you in color or in black and white, we can
slide the cels around to have pincers surround Warsaw or we can give
you full animation." [After Walt gave Frank an estimate of the production time,] Frank came back saying, "I won't get it for two weeks! Hell,
the entire maneuver only took thirty-six hours!"

After we finished *Moochie of the Little League*, Walt said, "We've got
to get some more. What can we get Ellis Marcus onto?" We got into
Pop Warner football. Walt got a letter from Mr. Number One in the
East who said he was coming out and he would like to say hello. Walt
passed it right on to me. I felt that would be no problem if he wanted
to say hello; sometimes these things only last five minutes. [During the
meeting] I had to come back to my office to pick up something, and
when I got back, this guy's got papers all over the desk, selling Walt on
the virtues of Pop Warner football and how it's going to be just as big as
Little League and that he'd like to use Walt's name up at the top. Now,
goddammit, I am pissed off that he has taken advantage of me. I didn't
want to expose Walt to that, so when this guy left to use the bathroom,
I'm there with egg on my face. "Walt, I am so sorry—" He said, "Whitey,
calm down. I get letters. I have to meet people. I reply to almost every
letter. Some kid wants to know if Walt Disney will pay his tuition

through college. Or 'My grandfather needs another wooden leg, could you please pay for it?'" He really calmed me down. He said, "I have to listen to this stuff. I have to listen to everybody, but I think we can wrap this up easy enough." It was a side of Walt that I didn't realize.

One time he had me paged during one of our productions because the secretary didn't know where I was. I heard that page and I moved! "Hi, Walt." I'm breathing hard. He says, "What the hell are you breathing hard for?" "Well, I came up here to—" "Goddammit, Whitey, I don't want to ever see you run." "Okay." "I know I can give you a sack and you'll run with it, but I want you to open the sack and look at it, because it might be full of shit!" "Okay, Walt, I'll come in breathing normally and not run." There was something thrilling that Walt—even my own dad wouldn't say that—but it touched me now to think about it.

DP: It was a special consideration.

LD: It was a relationship that was great. I remember one time we were talking about peddling papers. "You know, Whitey, I had my route, too. I used to have to get out in the morning and there'd be snow in Kansas City, or it'd be raining, and I'd have to be there. I know what it is." He said, "You went to John Marshall?" I said, "Yeah, but I dropped out, though, Walt." He said, "That's one thing we have in common. I dropped out of high school, too." I didn't bring anything to him except my enthusiasm that he liked, that Ben liked, I think that everybody I worked with as their assistant liked, because whatever I was working on, this was the most important project in the studio. It may not have been, but to me it was. If I had an ace in my back pocket, God gave me that.

DP: It seems to me the common thing that you have and all these people have is a dedication to what the studio was doing that's so rare—not rare here, but rare in the whole business world.

LD: It's got to be so rare in the business world, because outside of lawyers and doctors who get their fee, there are damn few people who could say, "My God, I've got goose pimples. I'm on the lot. I'm being paid for working and doing this." I mean, you'd come back at night. When the picture was finished and we had an answer print, I was the one that got a dollar bill, and I had the print under my arm, and I'd go to the Alexander Theater [in Glendale], up to the projection room, and we'd have our preview. I didn't get involved in the discussions. There's the old line where somebody said, "Well, Walt, you've done it again." Well, I think if it was a turkey, something that didn't go over too good, Walt would give him the eyebrow. But those were thrilling days for a kid like me to have a print under my arm that's going to be previewed in a theater.

DP: Even to hear about it, it seems like it must have been really exciting.
LD: But great, great, great artists from Hugh Hennesy to Al Zimin, great layout men who had earned their spurs before they ever came to the studio, editorial cartoonists and designers and fine artists. Frenchy [Gilles de Trémaudan] did great Mickey animation in *Hawaiian Holiday* (1937) for Ben and me—just a super guy. And right next door to him was Bob Wickersham, and then next door to him at the old studio was Johnny Cannon.

You see, Walt's great gift was taking a guy like Ugo D'Orsi, a European painter-designer, and he learned animation. Walt had that gift. I think he could take twenty guys who were not in the business and [say], "Hey, you're inclined—" Whether it was publicity or whatever, he would utilize the talents that existed there. That was his super gift.

A real highlight was when we hired Ollie Wallace, the musician. Ollie did the score for *Dumbo* and did some super things. His only claim to fame that I could relate to was that he wrote "Hindustan" [a love song, 1918]. He had played the organ in silent movies. Little bantam rooster with crazy hair like [Leopold] Stokowski. I was the one designated to work with Ollie as Ben's assistant on *Mickey's Trailer*. He was going to do the music. I don't know what happened to Bert Lewis at that time, but Bert was gone. Ollie used to call me Huff 'n Puff, but we had a great rapport. We worked together on that picture. That was Ollie's first picture, and he did many, many scores after that. A tremendous character. He also wrote "Der Fuehrer's Face" [1942]. A lot of people don't know that Ollie sang that song. It was in [the television show] *Disney's Oscar Winners*, one of our highest-ranking shows this past season on NBC.

A good part of the schedule [of shows on NBC] are two-parters that I make up from features, cutting them down. Last season, we put on

The Parent Trap. They wanted to play it as a two-hour vertical, so we had to cut twenty-four minutes out of it. My editor, Bill Penguin, and myself, we'd get together—and there is some sacred footage in there, Don. [After it was broadcast], I walked in with Ron [Miller] on a Monday morning. We're talking about this and that. I said, "Well, wait a minute. You're either going to say it's a lousy job of pulling twenty-four minutes out or it's a good job." "No," Ron said, "it's a good job. I think it plays better now than when it was in the theater." I'm waiting for [*Parent Trap* director] Dave Swift, who is my friend, to call and say, "Who in hell over there cut that up?" but as it turned out, sometimes these old things will improve with some cutting.

DP: One of the things that has always fascinated me about Walt was how he could meet people and judge their talents sometimes better than they could.

LD: Look at Les Clark. He could draw Mickey Mouse a little bit [in the beginning], and then he developed that super animation on *The Band Concert* that will live forever. Les did such great work! But let's face it, he didn't come out of New York, having worked for [Max] Fleischer or somebody, like some of these guys who later came in. Al Eugster, Jimmy Culhane, Dick Huemer had already established themselves as pillars of animation, But they all had to tighten up their belt and go to art school. Then young guys like Freddy Moore were coming along that they couldn't hold a candle to—Bill Tytla, a truly great pillar of the industry in the contributions he made. You see, it breaks down to many people. I mean, Walt was the guy that said, "Let's do this or let's not do this," but it had to be done and it took people like Ben Sharpsteen. Ben and I worked together [during] the latter stages of the war when Walt thought he might like to get into doing commercial-type, institutional-type things. So by golly, the studio gets the Firestone Company's *Building a Tire*, and Ben is the producer. Then we worked on another for Autolite Spark Plugs. But then Walt said, "Wait a minute, let's do it our way. Why should we build a storyboard that looks like it'll work and then you take it back and they want something different." We had to change it; they're spending the money. Walt said, "Let's get out of it." But Ben had great leadership in doing all of the True-Life Adventures. All the way across the board. What a man.

DP: Just to jump back to an earlier comment, when you were working on *The Mickey Mouse Club,* was this after it had already started?
LD: Yes. There was a fellow that had my job as the associate producer by the name of Hal Adelquist. I was still up in Utah on a picture called *Perri* while that [program] started. That was just a bitch. Can you imagine five days a week? Sure, we used cartoons, and they had a serial and had different units. Hal did a good job—I cannot be critical of him—getting this thing [going] along and pulling all the ends together. I thought the guy was going to go on and on forever with it, which was fine, because, I mean, I had something else that I undoubtedly would have gone on to. Then Walt called us both in, Hal and myself, and told Hal in front of me, "You're no longer on it. Whitey's taking over. We're going to improve it and improve the breed." Hal had his problems—God, everybody has some problems—but it wasn't long that he was gone. [In an interview with a local television station,] I said in effect [that *The Mickey Mouse Club*] was great while it lasted, but it was complete trivia and nothing significant, I remember saying, was accomplished, except we filled up a hundred hours and then we repeated them.

DP: Well, I think for my generation, since we grew up with it, it is very nostalgic. When I walked in today, I was thinking that every time I walk by the corner of Mickey Avenue and Dopey Drive, all I see is a photo of Annette standing by the pole from my copy of *The Mickey Mouse Club Annual.* Those are such strong memories.
LD: For you, it would have stronger memories, but I think that age span is very narrow. I think some of the younger kids couldn't remember, and a year or two older—your older brother probably doesn't have the same attachment that you do today.

DP: I think it's fun to look back at it. Many people my age had different reactions to Jimmie Dodd. Some liked him and some didn't. I always bought everything he said. I thought he was great. I especially loved it when he would come out at the end and talk to us. Those always meant a lot.

LD: Yes. Do something good, and if you can't say something nice, don't say anything. Jimmie wrote most of those or adapted them to the show. Jimmie was a real kind guy. I have to admit, I got embarrassed when he'd say, "Why? Because we *like* you." But Jimmie was a good tennis player and a likable guy. You didn't know how old he was; [he had] a certain youthfulness. Roy [Williams] was himself, big old Roy. Then there was Bobby Amsberry, who was killed in an automobile accident.

DP: I don't remember him, but I have read about him.

LD: You would see him, for instance, on Circus Day. He would be the guy in the opening of the song who would be at the ticket booth selling tickets. Bobby also wrote a lot of the material and some of the songs. He was on the first year all the time, and then we'd see him if we had a Malt Shop hop or something in the Sweet Shop. He was part of our little stock company.

DP: When I was at Disneyland yesterday, I saw a scene from one of the first *Disneyland* television programs, where Walt is talking about building Disneyland, and you just look at him, and he is so believable. He came across so well.

LD: I'll tell you, he had that magic. I'd like to think [this interview] might be just a little bit unique, because I didn't come here as an artist or a musician but as a guy that wanted to do something for [Disney].

DP: That's probably the best quality to have.

LD: And with the enthusiasm that I told you about in the beginning. That's my ace. Nobody impresses me—Donn Tatum, Card [Walker], or Ron [Miller], because I've met the great man in my lifetime.

Joyce Belanger

Joyce Belanger began working at Disneyland before the park
opened in July 1955. Her first job with the Mark Twain Riverboat led to a long career with Walt's first Magic kingdom.
When I interviewed Joyce by telephone on March 13, 1985, she
was working at the Disneyland Hotel Monorail. She completed
her long tenure at Disneyland as a ticket seller at the main
entrance, where I am sure her warm engaging personality set
just the right tone for many guests as they began their day in
Disneyland.

DP: How did you happen to go to work at Disneyland?
JB: A neighbor of mine had read in the paper where Disneyland was
taking part-time workers, and we were both housewives. She said, "Gee,
that sounds great." She had to sort of talk me into it. But we came
down and we put our application in. I got the job, and she didn't. And I
thought, "Well, I can do it for a couple of months. It's been thirty years!"

DP: Was this prior to the park opening?
JB: Yes, a week and a half, ten days prior to the park opening.

DP: Where did you begin working?
JB: I began working at the Mark Twain [Riverboat].

DP: Were you working there on opening day?
JB: Well, on the main opening day, yes. I always think of opening day as the first day, when there wasn't really any ticket selling or anything like that going on. All the rides and everything were free.

DP: That was for the people who had worked on the park and friends of the studio?
JB: Well, and the celebrities, too.

DP: This was the one that was on television?
JB: Yeah.

DP: Do you have any particular memories of opening day?
JB: I always remember that I was out there the night before. It was really a mess, you know. There was paint all over, and tools, and drop cloths. The windows were still covered with paint. Everybody was running around. And there were knives and hammers. The ticket booth for the Mark Twain wasn't even half finished. And we thought, "My gosh! How are they going to be able to open it to the press and all the celebrities and everybody who's going to be here the following day?" So we came back the next morning, and it just sparkled. Everything was clean and beautiful, and it looked just simply great.

DP: They must have had an army in there during the night.
JB: They did. They worked all night up until, I guess, eight o'clock the next morning. But they got results. It looked great.

DP: While working at the park, did you ever have a chance to meet Walt Disney?
JB: Oh, yes.

DP: What were your impressions?

JB: Oh, I thought he was just great because he was such an easy person to talk to. He loved Disneyland a great deal. A couple of times when we were talking to him, I thought, "Here is a man that is one of the most honored men in the world, and you would never know it." And he really did have this childlike quality about him that came through. And of course, the children, they simply adored him. I mean, he was like the Pied Piper. He always treated them so nicely.

DP: How have you managed to keep your excitement and retain the Disney spirit over all that time?

JB: That's a funny question, but it's really been sort of easy for me, because I guess I believed in the place so much. I'm proud of the place in the first place, because it's always had such high standards. Secondly, I've seen so many people come through with such high hopes and such expectancy, and I know that they're going to enjoy it. So I'm happy about that, because I know they're going to like it. And then the next day, they often come to me and they say, "Gee, we had a great time yesterday." It's wonderful for families to come to, to enjoy together. I'll see a family perhaps with four generations in it, and there aren't that many places where this happens. Just the other day, I had a lady eighty-four years old come out. It's wonderful to see that. You know, we were speaking about Walt Disney a while ago. I saw him one time at the Golden Horseshoe. He was sitting in the box opposite me. And he had seen that show dozens of times. And yet looking at him, you'd have thought it was the first time, because he seemed to enjoy it so much.

DP: What are you doing currently?

JB: Right now, I'm working at the hotel monorail. I like that, because I get to talk to people every day from all over the world. On that first day that I was here, when the celebrities and everybody was here, I remember sitting next to Ronald Reagan at Carnation [Plaza] on Main Street. And looking back on that, it's funny to think that here he was going to be a future president of the United States.

DP: Do you see any key or main ingredient to Disneyland's success over the years?

JB: I think part of it is the Disney name, but you can't go on your name forever. I think it's sticking to high standards. I really do, because people feel free to leave their children here for the day and know that everything is going to be fine. I think part of it is the high standards.

DP: Looking back over these thirty years, are there any outstanding memories that come to mind?

JB: Oh, yes, there are a lot of wonderful outstanding ones, but one of them concerns Walt Disney. I was working down by the Matterhorn, and he was going around all by himself. He'd stop, and he'd look at each on the rides. He'd look it over and look it over from the outside. Then he'd turn, and he'd look at another one and so on and so forth. And it was the next day he went to the hospital. And so I felt that he was just saying good-bye, that he really loved the park.

DP: How do you feel about the future of Disneyland? I know there are lots of things coming up, the new Star Wars attractions and that kind of thing. Does it feel pretty solid to you?

JB: Oh, yeah. I just hope that they don't stray too far from Disneyland— you know, what it basically stands for. It's been a wonderful place to work. I love it. I still like people after all these years.

John Catone

John Catone, a native of Girard, Ohio, applied for a job at Disneyland in March 1955. On opening day, July 17, 1955, John was working on the Autopia attraction. His greatest claim to fame came when he donned a space suit and wandered through Tomorrowland to greet guests. When I interviewed John by telephone on March 13, 1985, he was the manager of communication Services at Disneyland. John died on April 7, 2005. His contributions to the Disneyland story are memorialized by a window bearing his name over the Mad Hatter shop in the town square on Main Street U.S.A.

DP: I understand that when you first worked at Disneyland, you had the privilege of being the Spaceman in Tomorrowland.
JC: Yes.

DP: That must have been quite an experience.
JC: It was.

DP: Was it pretty hot in that costume?

JC: Oh, yes. I'd stay in there about twenty-five or thirty minutes, depending on the heat. That thing weighed sixty-six pounds. It was made by Kaiser Aluminum. It was a Kaiser suit. I used to average about thirteen thousand pictures a day with children and adults.

DP: That's really something! I imagine you were really a celebrity to kids at that time.
JC: I was. It was quite an achievement for those kids to take a picture with a spaceman. Of course, today it doesn't sound like much.

DP: I was there in 1956, so I remember what it was like before all the space adventures. How did you happen to go to work for Disneyland?
JC: Well, I heard that they were taking applications, and I came down here in March of 1955 to put in an application. I was working in Long Beach at the time. I had been working as an assistant manager and head lifeguard of a swimming pool back east. So they called me up and I went down for an interview. After the interview, I accepted their job.

DP: Was your first assignment there with Tomorrowland?
JC: My first assignment was as a ride operator on the old Autopia freeway.

DP: Oh, the one without a track.
JC: I worked that for one week, and then Jack Reilly, who was our area manager, came out and asked me if I could fit into this space suit. At that time, you got somebody that fit the costume, not the costume to fit. I said, "Sure." He said, "It'd just be a couple of hours." It was for *Life* magazine. Well, I was in it for a little over two years.

DP: On opening day, were you working on Autopia?
JC: Yeah, I was working on Autopia.

DP: Do you remember anything special about that?
JC: Yeah, it was quite an ordeal for these children to come out here and drive their own cars. And it was amazing how many movie stars we had

out here. I had Eddie Fisher and Elizabeth Taylor. They were married then, and they brought their children out. Alan Ladd was out here with his family. Dean Martin was out here. It was a lot of fun. They enjoyed driving. Frank Sinatra and Sammy Davis Jr. It was really cute with their kids because they were bumping each other in the car. [Frank would] turn around and say something to Sammy, and Sammy'd say, "Yeah, but you gotta learn how to drive." Frank would say, "Yeah, but you bumped me." It was a lot of fun.

DP: That was a fun Autopia, because I remember it didn't have a track down the middle, so you could really bang around.
JC: We had the police cars, too, then.

DP: Oh, were there?
JC: Yeah, we had one going in front of twelve cars and one behind. And if they did something wrong, and we had to cite them, we wouldn't give them their little driver's license from Richfield. A little yellow license we issued out to all good drivers.

DP: Yeah, I'm sure I used to have one. It seems to me that you used to be able to get stuck up on top of the freeway and somebody would come out from the bushes and get you started again.
JC: We had people work out in what we called Timbuktu. If somebody got stuck or jammed in the curb or something, we'd jump on it and move the car out.

DP: When you were working there, did you have a chance to meet Walt Disney?
JC: I saw him daily. Matter of fact, I was working on the Matterhorn—this was after I'd come out of the space suit. I was foreman of the Matterhorn, and I was doing a book called *Know the Ropes of the Matterhorn* for the University of Disneyland. I was walking across the Tomorrowland area and somebody pulled the two books I had—*Third Man on the Mountain* [1959] and *Seeing the Alps* [perhaps *Walking in the Alps* by Kev Reynolds]—that I was going through so I could get some information.

Somebody pulled the books out from under my arms, and I turned around. I had a closed fist. I thought one of the employees was joking around. Here it was Walt! "Oh, no! Don't hit me!" Then he asked me what I was doing. I told him. Then he got the area assistant manager and he told him, "You'd better get somebody to open up the Matterhorn. John and I are going to sit here in front of [the] 20,000 Leagues [exhibit], so we can talk about the book." We were there about forty minutes, and he told me if I needed any help who to call and so forth. I thanked him very much. But that's the kind of a guy he was. He'd stop and talk to all the operators.

DP: After you worked in the space suit in Tomorrowland, what did you do then?
JC: I went back to operations. I don't know if you remember the film, *Forty Pounds of Trouble*, with Tony Curtis?

DP: Yes.
JC: I was in that when I was on the Matterhorn. That was a lot of fun, too. They really enjoyed it. As a matter of fact, that's the first thing that they ever did out here as far as filming. That was the only one.

DP: And you're currently working in communications?
JC: I'm the manager of Communications Services, which entails the telephones, the mailroom, the main files which house contracts and so forth out of the Legal Department, the records center, the forms control area, our copy equipment, microfilm equipment, microfiche equipment, and typewriters. So it's a complete service.

DP: How have you managed to keep your Disney spirit all these years?
JC: I think it is really knowing Walt Disney, knowing what he believed in. When he talked to you, you knew that the man had a deep feeling for what he was doing. I think keeping that in mind, and then we have an annual Club 55 get together every year. [The club is for] all of the employees who started in 1955. Right now there are thirty active employees. It's ironic because it's our thirtieth year—thirty of us left who are

active in Club 55. It just worked out that way. And then every five years, all the inactive retirees come in, too. I think each year when we have that, it rekindles—you know, we sit there and we talk about Walt, and we talk about the area and so forth. So, you keep that feeling—knowing the man and knowing what he believed in and then seeing what he really put together and made it work when everybody else thought it would be foolish. Those are the things that really keep me moving, knowing that Disneyland will always be here even though I'm gone.

DP: What do you think is the key or main ingredient to the success of Disneyland?
JC: I think it's in the one word *Disney*—the man himself—and I think if you tie *Disney* to the word *dream*, I think this is what people remember. When they come here and they find out—first of all, it's very clean, and I think that that's the main thing that they keep coming back [for], and I think the courtesy of the employees, knowing that they are very important people to them, they do pay their salaries—those are the things that I think have maintained the audience that we get.

Van France

Van France was born in Seattle, Washington, on October 3, 1912. After a series of jobs that provided training and experience in the fields of labor and industrial relations for General Dynamics and Kaiser Aluminum, Van joined Disney in March 1955. He worked at a variety of positions with Disneyland but is best known for founding the University of Disneyland, which over the years has turned Disneyland employees into cast members who exemplify Walt Disney's philosophy of creating happiness for park guests. Van retired in 1978, served as a consultant to the parks, and wrote an autobiography, *Window on Main Street: Thirty-five Years of Creating Happiness at Disneyland Park*. Van was named a Disney Legend in 1994 and died on October 13, 1999.

I interviewed Van on March 14, 1985, by telephone. He and I then developed a friendship with the Disneyland Alumni Club serving as a common bond. (I worked at Disneyland in the summer of 1982.) Over the years, we corresponded mostly by mail. Van always had different stationary and usually with a comical letterhead. His typewriter filled in some letters and had a peculiar mind of its own that seemed to fit Van. I never met him in person, but I knew from a distance that he was one of the special people that put the magic in Disneyland.

DP: How long did you work at Disneyland?
VF: Thirty years.

DP: How did you happen to go to work at Disneyland?
VF: The first vice president–general manager at Disneyland [C. V. Wood] was a man I'd worked with before in Texas, and then we'd done some consulting work together. He had been with Stanford Research [Institute]. Walt retained him to be vice president–general manager. Then finally about six months before opening, they found out that they needed a training program, so he knew that I had done that sort of thing and retained me on a consulting basis. Then I stayed around.

DP: Did you work with the training program during your entire career at Disneyland?
VF: Well, I sort of set up what is called the University of Disneyland. I sort of set up the first orientation program.

DP: I was really impressed with the orientation program when I went through it. It was quite extensive and made me feel part of the whole team right from the beginning.
VF: When you went through, it was probably a little bit more sophisticated than when we started out. But it's still a good program.

DP: Were you working in that capacity when the park opened—the first day and the first summer?
VF: Yeah, 1955. I was on a contract at that time, a week-to-week contract to organize the orientation and training program and to set it up.

DP: During the time you worked there, I'm sure you had a chance to meet Walt Disney?
VF: Yes.

DP: Can you tell me what your impressions were of him?
VF: I thought he was a sensational man, really, one of the most important people in my life. I didn't work for him directly. I usually worked for

somebody that worked directly for him, but I did know him. In fact, I'd write my handbooks pretty much with him in mind, because he had a good sense of humor and had his own idea of what he was doing. I think he was a genius of a type.

DP: I would agree with you there. What would you see as the key or main ingredient to Disneyland's success?
VF: There are so many of them. In the first place, I'm quite prejudiced— I'm catholic in my tendencies, you see—because Disneyland itself is the one place in the world that Walt personally designed and then had maybe eleven years to work around and form it, so I use the expression that it's the roadmap of Walt Disney's life or mind. So just the basic design, the detail, and everything else is one thing. We had a lot of comments from people who said they would come back because the people were so friendly and the place was so clean. So you have this personal design. And Walt was there, you know. He walked over every foot, so it was molded by him and then the people—we invest an awful lot in the attitudes of our people and in the cleanliness of the park.

DP: Looking back over the years, are there any outstanding memories that you have from 1955 to the present at Disneyland?
VF: Yeah. Everybody has a lot of them, you know. My general philosophy is that you gotta look ahead. You can glance in the rearview mirror, but you better keep your eyes on where the hell you're going, you know.

DP: Along that vein, how would you see the future of Disneyland?
VF: I'm very bullish about it right now. Nineteen-eighty-four was a hell of a year, if you followed the history of Disney. People were trying to buy us out, we had a change in top management, but now we have a very aggressive top management in [Michael] Eisner and [Frank] Wells, and that sort of thing. Hopefully, they'll come up with some movies that will then help Disneyland. You see, the last blockbuster movie we had was *Mary Poppins*, and *Mary Poppins* made enough money, as Walt said, to pretty much pay for the Pirates of the Caribbean, New Orleans Square, the Haunted Mansion, and a few other things.

DP: From what I've read, it sounds like the next addition may come from outside of Disney, with the George Lucas attraction themed to *Star Wars*.

VF: That's what I gather. Personally, I hope that nothing really changes much on Main Street or in most of the place—it's like the Vatican, you know. If attendance drops off at the Vatican, they're not going to take out Michelangelo and put in Andy Warhol! But Tomorrowland— the world changes so rapidly that it's almost impossible not to have it Todayland. So I'm very optimistic that we'll come up with some stuff in Tomorrowland that will make it very, very exciting.

DP: That seems to me, too, to be the area where you could have the most changes, because there are so few attractions that I think attendance has dropped off. One of the attractions I worked on was Mission to Mars. It didn't seem to be as popular as some of the other ones.

VF: Mission to Mars, you know, was a warmed-over—when we first opened, we had the Rocket to the Moon, and, by God, we got to the moon before Sputnik! We could see [Sputnik] go by from a bar across the street. At that time, it was a pretty progressive idea, but, my God, that's one of the problems: you start in planning something, and by the time you get it done, it's a couple or three years, and by that time, the world has changed so damn fast.

DP: I just read yesterday that Tomorrowland was originally supposed to be 1986, so we've almost caught up to the original Tomorrowland.

VF: We're past it!

Bobby Burgess

Bobby Burgess was born in Long Beach, California, on May 19, 1941. He started dancing as a young child and made it his life's work. He appeared in many amateur events and contests before an agent brought him to the Disney Studios for what became a series of auditions, first for the Spin and Marty serial and then for the role of a Mouseketeer on *The Mickey Mouse Club*. Bobby was featured for the entire run of that program, frequently partnered with Sharon Baird, Annette Funicello, and Jimmie Dodd in dance routines. After the show ended, Bobby returned to public school in Long Beach and eventually attended California State University at Long Beach. After winning a dance contest, Bobby joined *The Lawrence Welk Show* in 1961 and remained a cast member for twenty-one years, and he has subsequently continued his show business career. I interviewed him at his home on April 5, 2005. I really enjoyed meeting and talking with Bobby. He was very likable, an easy conversationalist, positive, enthusiastic, and sincere—just what I would expect from a former Mouseketeer.

DP: I've read you started dancing when you were about three or four?
BB: Yeah, I used to twirl around with the music on the radio, and my parents thought, "This boy seems to have rhythm," and so they gave

me tap dancing lessons. I had my first partner at five, and we broke up
at eight, and I thought, "I'm destined to be [part of] a dance team," so
on *The Mickey Mouse Club* it was Bobby and Sharon, and on *The Lawrence Welk Show*, Bobby and Mira, and Bobby and Cissy, and Bobby
and Elaine. But, yeah, I started by taking tap dancing, which my folks
thought [was] a guy's dance. They were right. And then I branched out
at about eleven or twelve, doing jazz, and then I started taking ballroom
dancing and then putting in some ballet and a little bit of everything
and taking some singing [lessons]. When I was thirteen, I auditioned for
the show.

DP: And you did all this while living in Long Beach?
BB: Yeah, in Long Beach.

DP: So you were really outside of the Hollywood world, while a lot of the
kids who appeared on *The Mickey Mouse Club* lived in the San Fernando
Valley.
BB: But I had a mom that would drive me up to South-Central [Los
Angeles], where there was a great black tap dancing teacher named
Willie Covan who had taught Ann Miller and Donald O'Connor and
others. And then she would take me up to Louis DaPron in Beverly
Hills and B. B. Carpenter on Slauson Avenue. So I was taking stuff here,
there, and everywhere.

DP: I know you mentioned that it was quite a sacrifice for her to drive
you up to film *The Mickey Mouse Club* all the time.
BB: Yeah, because there were no freeways then. Five trips from Long
Beach, an hour each way by Western Avenue, was kind of a long trek.
Finally the Santa Ana, the first freeway, got built. I remember we used to
go via Downey to pick up Dennis Day and his mother because she didn't
drive, so we would pick up Dennis just about every day and take him
with us.

    I have two sisters and a brother. My dad was a meat cutter, and he
worked nine to five and my mother was a stay-at-home 1950s mom, and
at that time, when I first signed for Disney, which was at $120 a week, I

was making more than my dad [made in] a week. At that time we didn't know anything about contracts, so, of course, Disney got all merchandising rights and all tour rights. Wherever we'd go touring, it was just part of the deal. Even Disneyland, we'd go out on the weekends; we'd work Monday through Friday [at the studio], then maybe Saturday and Sunday, we'd do two or three shows out at Disneyland, which was fun because we were kids and loved what we did.

But anyway, I danced everywhere—I mean, every Lions Club and Elks Club and county fair, the L.A. County Fair, and all these places, and then all of a sudden in the 1950s these amateur TV shows got going. And you could win all kinds of loot. They didn't pay you anything, but, I mean, I won my first bike, and I won my first aquarium, and I have four aquariums still going after all these years. So that was probably 1953 or something like that. That got me going with that. And I won my folks a washer and dryer. That was great back then.

DP: Those are big prizes.

BB: So I did seventy-five of those shows, and it was all loot. Then an agent saw me on one, and she called the station. I had won the show that night, and she called and said, "I can get that boy some professional work." So then she started sending me out, and the first thing I went out on, I got, so that really encouraged her. It was a toothpaste commercial with Ozzie and Harriet [Nelson], and I went to school with Rick Nelson, and Ozzie directed me. That was for Listerine toothpaste. So that was fun. And then I did some episodic [television] things and a few things here and there. But then when I was thirteen, she sent me out to Disney. And I'm sure that's one of your questions, "How did you get the job?"

DP: I'd like to hear that story. One of the things I'd like to ask you about—and I think this is probably in contrast to some of the other Mouseketeers—is that you had said somewhere that it was your decision all the way. I mean, your parents didn't push you to do this show.

BB: I just loved to dance, and it was always so much fun to me—you know, just to get out there and hoof away or whatever. And I think you'll find the same with Sharon. She just loved to dance. But that was my first big thing, getting on *The Mickey Mouse Club*.

DP: You said that was why you were smiling so much.

BB: And I was just going crazy that first year. Luckily, by the third year I was a cool adolescent, and I had settled down, and I was like everybody, kind of got cool and sharp. Like Darlene [Gillespie], she was pigtails and freckles [at the start], and by the time the third year came around, she was blond with false eyelashes and had a sexy voice. You know what I mean?

DP: She had a very mature voice. I was listening to some recordings of her and she had a beautiful voice.

BB: To me, she was the most talented Mouseketeer overall. I mean, she was a comedian, she sang great, she danced great. In fact, after *The Mickey Mouse Club*, she really got serious with her ballet and was on toe and doing all kinds of stuff, and then, you know, she changed her name to Darlene Valentine and became a country singer. I don't know if she moved to Nashville. I think she did. She did some recording. But there was the Annette charisma that came across, and everybody will tell you that it was the audience that discovered her, but, of course, Walt Disney discovered her. But she always said to everybody, "Well, I didn't really sing and dance that great," so I don't know. She was just so natural, and she had sex appeal. Plus I think she was the first Mouseketeer to blossom, so to speak. Do you know what I mean?

DP: I do! Just to jump back to when you came to *The Mickey Mouse Club* audition: What was that like?

BB: You know, I can remember that first audition like it was yesterday. It was really, really, really hot. We were outside with our parents, outside the soundstage. I can just remember how hot it was. Because it was Burbank in, was it May or June? Well, anyway, it was just so hot, and we went in, and actually we got individual auditions. I think I did "Blue Skies," which was a tap dance I had learned that had lots of taps—pretty hot for a kid who's thirteen. But my gimmick was my "Rock around the

Clock," my barefoot jazz dance, because rock was just coming in—it was 1955 and Bill Haley and the Comets [were very popular]. And so that was something different. But I went through five auditions. I remember one time I came back and it was Jack Lavin, Lee Traver, Hal Adelquist, and Dik Darley, and then it was Walt Disney with everybody at the very end. And they would line up different groups, which was weird, in the soundstage where we eventually recorded all the stuff. And they would say, "Okay, here's these eight, and then here's these eight kids. Now, this one, Cubby [O'Brien], plays great drums, and this one is a really an outstanding dancer, but he sings too." And that would be me, you know. "And this one is really cute," and it was Bronson [Scott] or it was Karen [Pendleton] or whoever. So there were twenty-four [Mouseketeers] the first year, which people don't realize; they just know the roll-call kids. [Those Mouseketeers who were identified by Jimmie Dodd in a roll call.] Basically through the first years, they just knew the nine of us pretty much [Bobby, Annette Funicello, Darlene Gillespie, Tommy Cole, Doreen Tracey, Karen Pendleton, Cubby O'Brien, Sharon Baird, and Lonnie Burr].

DP: So when you went back for these five auditions, did you think after the first one that you might get this, or were you worried because you kept having to go back, or was each one encouraging?

BB: No, encouraging. I told you the very first thing I went out for was the Spin and Marty serial. They had all these guys. And I thought, "Well, I've done some acting," and I'd taken some acting lessons since I was four or five years old along with everything else. So I read, and it was fine. They said, "Do you sing and dance?" and I said, "Well, that's mainly what I do." And they said, "Well, down the hall at two o'clock we're having Mouseketeer auditions." So I did my tap dance there. But the main audition I remember was that hot day where we were all standing outside on the asphalt.

But no, each one was encouraging, and then at the very end I got it. But so many of them moved to Hollywood U.S.A. And a lot of the moms and dads actually used the kids' money to enhance their lifestyle or even live on it. Some built swimming pools or bought new houses with their Mouseketeer money. Mine didn't touch a penny. And my mom said, "I don't want to move away from Long Beach." My dad had the job with Safeway that he'd had all of his life. In fact, when he retired at sixty-five, he had the record for all of the Safeway stores for never missing a day for being sick. So he was always real loyal and always did his job. So no, she didn't want me to be the Hollywood kid like so many. And you know the famous story about how Walt Disney used to take everybody around the neighborhood and say, "See those [kids] over there? That's what I want to be Mouseketeers," and the producers or whoever he had with him would say, "Well, what do you mean?" And he said, "I don't want those slick professional kids, I want the kids next door." Of course, we had to learn how to sing and dance and do that whole bit. But he didn't want the phony voices and that kind of thing. He wanted to make everybody think that they could be Mouseketeers.

DP: Which we all did. I mean, that was part of the allure. We all sat there with our ears on.

BB: I kind of think the way they did it was the right way if they wanted that because pretty much they got kids and amateurs who hadn't done much. Now, Sharon had and Lonnie had—just a few. Even Darlene and Doreen and some of them just came from Burch Mann's dancing school, and Darlene sang with a trio, but they had her come out and sing by herself. But they were amateurs coming in fresh, so you know we had all that enthusiasm. In my case, because I did those seventy-five amateur TV shows, I was so glad to get a paying job.

You know, one thing I always say is I was lucky to go from one family institution to another, from Walt Disney to Lawrence Welk. I learned my discipline from *The Mickey Mouse Club*. I learned to be prepared and to be on time and to not touch the props and have respect for the people who are doing their job. That was taught to me on *The Mickey Mouse Club*, and then when I got on the Welk show, Lawrence Welk used to say, "I never have any trouble with Bobby because he was raised by Walt Disney." I mean, that was such a great thing to say and a funny thing to say. But it's true.

DP: What do you remember about the first day, once you got the job?

BB: It was all done on that big orchestra stage. It was done where we actually recorded the music. It was all done on that stage, and the auditioning, too. Then, of course, the filming was done at Stage [2]. And then the [school] trailer was parked right there. I don't know—it was a really unique experience. It was really, really fun.

DP: Somewhere you had said it made you feel small to be on this huge soundstage.

BB: Even where everything was [recorded] had a huge tall ceiling. I just remember when we were actually filming the first time, the lighting was interesting because we had a cameraman named Gordon Avil and he was actually telling us about lighting. In those days, they had what they call the central arc, and you would hear it go, and then you would feel this big main light on you, and you knew that you had to be in this light, and I think a few of them learned how to cast shadows on the other ones. And then you were learning about all of these different things. I became friends with all the crew, too.

I was fourteen, so I must have auditioned before my birthday—like the beginning of May—and so we probably started filming in June. We filmed all that summer. So I was filming from fourteen to seventeen and then I went back to my high school and graduated as a senior.

DP: I know some people had problems returning to public schools. Was that particularly hard for you?

BB: No, it was fine. I had a lot of my same friends. You know, I'd walk down the hall, and my name had changed to Mickey—"Hey, Mickey!" You know, that kind of thing, but that didn't bother me.

DP: And how about college?

BB: I thought I needed to get back to trying to be a little bit of a normal guy even though I was in show business and taking dancing lessons. At nineteen I got the Welk show. But I went to Cal State–Long Beach and got in a fraternity, Sigma Pi. It was a real great and real friendly active chapter at Cal State–Long Beach in those days. I was a theater arts major and a Spanish minor.

DP: One of the people I wanted to ask you about was Jimmie Dodd. I know you met him at the audition, and I think you had said on one of the shows that one of your favorite things from *The Mickey Mouse Club* was the father-son dance number you two did.

BB: Jimmie was just this really special guy. The good thing was that he wasn't partial—I mean, he made all the kids feel special, like they were all really equal.

DP: And that's how it felt to us watching, that he treated everybody the same.

BB: But in my case, especially after the show, in [May] 1959 and 1960, I was the only one that didn't have a parent going to Australia [on the Mouseketeers' tours of the country], because my mom was still with my brother and sisters. I was eighteen or nineteen. I was right at that point where I was trying to get my own head together. So I didn't really want my mom to go. But the littler kids needed [a parent]. The first one I was really in "love" with was *Sheena [Queen] of the Jungle* [played by Irish McCalla], who went with us. But anyway, Jimmie and Ruth [Dodd] kind of took me over, and that's when this real Mousekeson/Mousekedad [relationship] came into being. They threw a big birthday party every year, because I was over there for my eighteenth and nineteenth birthday, and all the little Australian girls in those days sent boys handkerchiefs. I got about a hundred handkerchiefs those two years, and koala bears and boomerangs and all kinds of stuff. But Jimmie and Ruth kind of watched out for me. And then he got me going to the Hollywood Christian group.

DP: I remember Roy [Williams] mentioning it. It was something Roy Rogers and Dale Evans were part of.

BB: Yeah, and Ethel Waters would sing at it. I don't know if he started it, but he was real instrumental in a thing called the Share the Blessings Brunch at the Beverly Hilton. Jimmie was always real active, maybe even in charge of that, and so he would invite me to that. But Jimmie never forced his religion onto you. I mean, it was just a thing that he mentioned—"Hey would you be interested in coming to our group? We're getting together on Saturday night." But you've got to remember that Jimmie and Ruth had no children, so we were almost like his Mousekekids—all of us, in a way.

DP: As a kid watching the show, I really liked his little "Doddisms" at the end where he would come out and talk. I know some of my friends thought they were corny, but I really bought into them. And when I watch some of the old shows, I still like to hear them. There are still some good lessons in what he said.
BB: I watched that DVD of the first week [of *The Mickey Mouse Club*] and I can't remember if he used cue cards or not. It sure looks like he is very natural. Jimmie looks like he is really talking to you. I can't remember if they had a teleprompter. I don't even know if they were invented by then.

DP: So his death was like losing an older brother?
BB: No, it was more like losing a dad.

DP: When you were at Disneyland on opening day, after you came out and did your introductory dance, I guess you moved into the parade. Was that really exciting being there?
BB: Yeah, it was, because nobody knew who we were. So we were just some kids dancing and singing, and a lot of them had the [prop] horses. I think it was Lonnie who hated being on the horse. Luckily, I was dancing jitterbug with Sharon, so I didn't have to be on the horse. But anyway, when we were in the parade, I had a horse for that. But it was one of those really hot days, and we had wool outfits on, and the pavement was soft, and there were hardly any drinking fountains.

DP: Did you know Walt Disney very well?
BB: We didn't work with him much. One of my favorite things to do would be at breaks to go over and watch him film because he was on the

next stage, and it was real eerie because it was pitch-black. All [that was lighted was] his little set, with him sitting there. And, you know, he was good. He did first takes and was so natural, being from Missouri and all. We knew him, but we always said he was like a principal of a school. He wanted us to call him Uncle Walt, but he was always Mr. Disney because we were 1950s kids, and we respected our elders and all. So I don't know, you just didn't know what to say to him. In my case, I always thought I wasn't a pushy kid, so I wouldn't go up and say, "Hi, Mr. Disney." I would actually almost go the other way when I'd see him coming. But they say you would see him in the back of the studio watching us film, and they say he watched all of our dailies and made suggestions about who to keep and who not. And I did go up to his office just to go exploring around, and outside his office was a storyboard of the next day's [filming of the] *Mickey Mouse Club*, and it would be Bobby and Sharon doing a jitterbug dance, and there would be ears and teeth and movement and dust flying everywhere, that kind of thing. So you knew that in the next day or two you would be doing a jitterbug dance of some kind or whatever kind of dance they wanted you to do because you were storyboarded.

DP: It almost sounds like a Roy Williams storyboard.

BB: It probably was, because it looked like his stuff. You know, his triangle face and all the things that he did and that kind of thing.

What was always fun was performing with Annette, because she became so popular. And then Jimmie Dodd wrote the Annette song, and then I got to dance a ballet with her and lift her around. But it was hard to do lifts with her, because she was very girly and very weak and had little fine features. So I'd put her on my shoulder, and she ended up laughing so hard that I dropped her, and then she would laugh and laugh, lying on the floor. Yeah, that was always fun. And we were always the tallest, we were always in the back. So, then, pretty much if I wasn't with Sharon, I was with Annette.

DP: When you got to the end of the show, when you knew it was going to end, was that traumatic, or did you feel you were ready to move on?

BB: I know the girls always tell how they cried and that kind of thing. You felt bad, but I don't know, I kind of wanted to go on with my life and do something else. Only Cubby and I were on roll call every year for the boys—Tommy was not the first year, and Lonnie was not the last year. And there were five girls that were on all of it. So I was really in there especially with the Mouseketeers doing everything that they did. And they really kept us busy.

DP: Did you go up to Walt Disney's apartment above the firehouse the first day?

BB: No, but we did get passes so we could get in the front of all the rides, which was really a dream come true for a kid. Especially, you know, if it was the [Mad Hatter] teacups that we really wanted to go on, and Dumbo, and a few things like the jungle ride. But I don't remember ever seeing that apartment until about three years ago when I did an event at Club 33 [a members-only club in Disneyland] where I spoke. I think it was with Sherry [Alberoni], and they gave all those people—I don't remember why it was such a special event—a special tour of that apartment. So that was kind of neat.

DP: You were at Disneyland when the president of Indonesia was visiting there?

BB: Yeah, Sharon and I, I think it was the first year, went out and took his son on Autopia and rode the train. And Walt Disney was there, because he was showing President Sukarno around, and we were right there. And then I remember we got to meet the emperor of Japan, too. They were guests out there. But that was a special one because we were right there with them. So that was kind of a nice little perk.

DP: You said that when Walt was alive, you used to walk down Main Street and look at the firehouse, hoping to see him, and that you still do that sometimes now when you are there.

BB: I think about it.

Every year the Welk show played Harrah's Club at Tahoe. I drove up for [one] year, and for some reason I was all by myself. So I'm thinking I've got some time, and it's not too late. It's just starting to get dark, but it's okay. So I go off maybe three or four miles down this little side road to Devil's Post Pile. It's these strange [natural] formations. So I go up there on this little dirt trail. I'm coming down, and nobody's there, nobody but me, and I'm thinking, "Gosh, I better get going, it's starting to get dark." Up this trail comes this little old man, bent over, smoking a cigarette, with his hat pulled down. And I pass him, and it's like I almost do a movie double take. And I said, "Walt Disney." And he said, "Mouseketeer Bobby." I said, "What are you doing here?" He said, "I bought this cabin for my daughter, Diane, probably ten years ago, because she wanted to ski at Mammoth. And I've never seen it, so I thought, 'I'm going to see that cabin. While I'm here I'm going take a little walk and see Devil's Post Pile.'" I had to be up there in June. So that was probably six months before he died. That's when I saw him last. That's very eerie, isn't it?

DP: Yeah, it is. Especially just to see him out by himself like that in the middle of nowhere.

BB: And that we recognized each other. I didn't have to say, "Hi, remember me, I'm Mouseketeer Bobby." And we probably hadn't seen each other for a few years, because I left the show in 1958.

DP: But even the fact that you recognized him, that you could see enough of him—

BB: Yeah, I remember it was a blue hat, one of those funny little fisherman hats.

DP: When you met him when you were a kid, do you remember your impressions of him?

BB: No, except it seemed to me he was real dressed up. Didn't he always get dressed up? Seems like I always saw him dressed up. Maybe I'm thinking of seeing him on the television show. But even when he would come down the street—it seems to me he would walk right down the middle of the street—I always saw him dressed up. Even at the final audition when I saw him, he wore a coat and tie and the whole bit. I didn't kibitz with him or talk to him or anything.

DP: Did you talk to him when you did the fourth anniversary show of the *Disneyland* television series or when he was there on the set? Some Mouseketeers say he was there all the time, and some say he was hardly ever there.

BB: I think you would see him occasionally, but not that much. He was so busy. Disneyland was just opening. Our show was going. *Lady and the Tramp* and *Sleeping Beauty* were happening—a million things happening all of a sudden at the studio. So he was really busy. And he was doing [the television program] *Disneyland* too. He was doing those introductions. He was spread pretty thin at that time.

DP: When he died, do you remember your reaction?

BB: No, it was just real sad. I think it was probably lung cancer, wasn't it? I know he was a heavy smoker, but he never let us see him smoke. You know, back in those days, you worried about your reputation. Nobody did anything. You didn't even want people to see you smoke. I never smoked anyway. I'm sure he thought [that] especially around kids you don't want to have them see you smoke. He was a nice guy.

DP: How was Roy Williams to work with?

BB: Oh, I thought he was funny. He came up with funny ideas. He didn't sing or dance, but he was such an interesting contrast because he was the big Mooseketeer. He was big and heavy. But he loved doing it, and he'd been a gagman at Disney Studios since the 1930s, and they say he invented the ears because in one cartoon Mickey takes them off or something.

DP: It's in *Karnival Kid* (1929). Mickey tips his ears to Minnie. What was production coordinator Hal Adelquist like?

BB: A real friendly, down-to-earth kind of guy. He's the one that always had a birthday party for you and had a special cake made for you. He was real hands-on the first year. So we saw mostly [director] Dik Darley and Hal Adelquist and a little bit of [producer] Bill Walsh, and the other guy that we'd see sometime was Bill Anderson. He was above Bill, so he was even more remote. And then there was Walt.

DP: Somewhere you said, "I felt like I needed to live up to the reputation of being a Mouseketeer and representing Walt Disney." Has that been kind of a guiding thing for you in some ways in your life?

BB: I went from this family show to the other big family show. But I don't know, I just think my parents raised us right; you know, it's just kind of like the Disney touch. All of us original Mouseketeers pretty much came out pretty good. It was like we were expected to have certain standards working for the company, and Lawrence Welk was the same.

DP: How would you like people to remember Walt Disney?

BB: Well, it was mainly that he did so much for family entertainment and, of course, animation. He brought it out with *Snow White and the Seven Dwarfs*. He just created that whole genre. And then the amusement parks. I have been to that little amusement park over where the Beverly Center is when it was just a nothing, with little ponies and little baskets and stuff. And I read that that's where he got the idea for Disneyland. Well, look what Disneyland started. So he did not reinvigorate [theme parks] because there wasn't anything, but he created all these things. You know what I always remember too? How EPCOT was supposed to look. Remember it was a dome? It was going to be thirty-five or forty thousand people living in there, and even the air was going to be piped in or fresh.

But I guess he died too soon. Maybe it could have happened. He was so progressive [in his] thinking. Even with *The Mickey Mouse Club*, he was so interested in things like outer space. I can remember meeting Wernher von Braun, and he was walking down the street and talking to us. But I mean, you know, [Walt] was real, and then think about all his True-Life Adventures that were so popular back then. Nobody was doing that then: *The African Lion* (1955) and *Secrets of Life* (1956) and all those great films. Such an imagination. But now you wonder, where's it going? Who's going to do it?

DP: Big shoes to fill.

BB: So much has become corporate. I mean, when we used to work at Harrah's, Bill Harrah was the same, the way he treated you. He gave the stars a house with a custom Rolls [Royce] to drive, and he lived right on the lake. And he gave you boat rides in this huge boat and would take you over to Emerald Bay and feed you these great sandwiches, and we'd go skiing. I mean, it was the same idea, and look how successful Harrah's became. And then he passed away, and somebody took it over, and now it's just a business—sold all those houses, and all those perks are gone. And you wonder now, is Disney just going to become another big perk studio? You hope not, because it was so innovative.

Sharon Baird

Sharon Baird was born on August 16, 1943, in Seattle, Washington. Like her frequent Mouseketeer partner, Bobby Burgess, Sharon began dancing as a young child, and her skills as a dancer defined her show business career. After winning the Little Miss Washington State contest, she came to California with her parents for the Little Miss U.S.A. contest. Sharon remained in California and turned professional, with television appearances on *The Colgate Comedy Hour*, *The Damon Runyon Theatre*, *Death Valley Days*, and *The Donald O'Connor Show* as well as movie appearances, most notably dancing with Dean Martin in *Artists and Models*. Sharon was a featured Mouseketeer for the entire run of *The Mickey Mouse Club*, appearing in many memorable dance routines and in the serial, Annette. Sharon continued her show business career both onstage and in television with series such as *The World of Sid and Marty Krofft* and *The New Zoo Revue*. Ironically, Sharon appeared in the film *Ratboy* in 1986. Sharon continues to be very active in and out of the world of show business.

I interviewed Sharon on April 10, 2005, at her home. Sharon's mother, Nikki, was delightful and greeted me as we were introduced with "Hey there! Hi there! Ho here!" from "The

Mickey Mouse Club March." I really enjoyed talking with Sharon. She, like Bobby, was very positive and enthusiastic and a lot of fun, the perfect representative of the female Mouseketeers.

DP: From what I've read, I guess you and Lonnie were the two more professional kids to try out for *The Mickey Mouse Club*.

SB: Right. Lonnie and I had actually worked together before *The Mickey Mouse Club* on *The Colgate Comedy Hour*. I was under contract to Eddie Cantor, and I did his show every month.

DP: And your legs were insured?

SB: Yes, I insured my legs for fifty thousand dollars. Actually, when I went out to interview for Eddie Cantor, they had a sketch for two little girls and two little boys to dance on the show. And I was too small, but they liked my dancing, so they wrote in a special part for me afterwards. And after the show aired, Eddie Cantor's attorney called my folks and said that he wanted to sign me under contract.

DP: How long had you been dancing before the contract?

SB: I started dancing when I was three. My parents used to go square-dancing at night when I was real young. And I would want to go, too, and they would say, "No, you're too young to go." Well, to shut me up, they would say, "If you stay with the babysitter tonight, we'll take you to your own dancing lessons." So they took me to a little dancing school in the neighborhood. The day I went to watch, they had been working all year for a recital that was going to be held in six weeks. [The instructor] said, "You can start in six weeks, but why don't you sit down and watch." So I did, and I was patting my foot. She said, "You want to get up and try?" And I got up and did it, and I was in the recital six weeks later.

DP: And you won the Little Miss Washington contest?

SB: Little Miss Washington State.

DP: And that brought you to California?

SB: Right, to compete for Little Miss U.S.A. I came in second. My parents had been living in Seattle, and it was too dreary for my dad—there wasn't enough sunshine. So they moved to California. I grew up in Van Nuys, and I was living in Van Nuys when I did *The Mickey Mouse Club*.

DP: And your dad worked for Flying Tigers?
SB: In Seattle, he worked for Boeing, and then Flying Tigers when he first moved to California. Then he went to work for Lockheed for a long time.

DP: Did you do some episodes of *Death Valley Days* before *The Mickey Mouse Club*?
SB: I did. [Also] *The Damon Runyon Theatre* I did with John Ireland. And *The Donald O'Connor Show*. Donald O'Connor—what a wonderful man he was—extremely talented.

DP: I understand your first movie was *Bloodhounds of Broadway* with Mitzi Gaynor.
SB: Right. With Mitzi Gaynor and Scott Brady. She was a delight. I just loved her.

DP: And then *Artists and Models* was the next?
SB: Yes, Dean Martin and Jerry Lewis, before they split up.

DP: How were they to work with?
SB: Great. Dean Martin was so much fun to work with. We sang and danced. And then actually I was prerecording a song that we were doing in the movie at Capitol Records, and Jimmie Dodd was there doing a recording session, and he saw me and recommended me to the Disney Studios.

DP: At the time of the audition for *The Mickey Mouse Club*, did you want to be a Mouseketeer?
SB: I didn't know what a Mouseketeer was. None of us knew what a Mouseketeer was. Actually, my agent didn't want me to, because people

were calling her and requesting me by name, so she didn't want me to go out for *The Mickey Mouse Club*. What she agreed to was a serial, When I Grow Up [What I Want to Be] with a [teenager learning to be a] stewardess, [but] they wanted little blond girls with freckles, and that, of course, wasn't me. But she sent me out for that hoping it would just be [okay], and I actually auditioned for *The Mickey Mouse Club* there. I wanted to do it because I loved to sing and dance, and that's exactly what it was. Also the beauty of it—and my mother came up with this—[was] that working for Disney on *The Mickey Mouse Club*, we were allowed to be ourselves, which is what they wanted. The other things that I did, I was in an adult world playing a part.

DP: In your audition, you sang a song called "I Didn't Know the Gun Was Loaded"?
SB: Yes, with my jump rope. First it was a lariat, and I danced, spinning the lariat, and then I put it down into a jump rope and I would jump rope, tap dance double time to the music.

DP: Did you have one audition, or did you have to come back?
SB: I think I went back a couple of times.

DP: You have said that one of the best questions people have asked you is this: Are you the way you are because you worked at Disney, or did you work at Disney because of the way you are? I like that question.
SB: I do too. And the answer is both, I'm sure. The other studios were more like a factory. At Disney Studios, I mean, there were flowers and plants, and all the streets were named after characters, and there was a lawn, and there was a baseball diamond and ping-pong tables, and Walt Disney never let anyone swear around us. And in your contract, you couldn't do anything that was not Disney, the Disney image. I just think you acquire that in your working there. But then again, you were hired because of who you were, too.

DP: Part of the appeal of the show was that you were all yourselves, and I think for us watching it at home, it made us feel more a part of it.

SB: Well, that was Walt Disney's idea. He didn't want a slick nightclub routine. He wanted the kids next door that would be playing in the playground.

DP: I think that worked well.
SB: They kept a lot of mistakes in, unless it was something drastic, you know. You'd be on the wrong foot or turn in the wrong direction. Kids do that.

DP: You were at Disneyland on opening day?
SB: We came out of the Mickey Mouse Theater, and we all did our little dance, and then we did the parade. And little did we know then—I feel so honored—we were in the very first parade down Main Street at Disneyland. Who knew where that was going to go? Our show hadn't opened; we didn't know if we were going to be a success. We were just kids having a good time. So we did this parade, and at the end of the parade, they took us all up to Walt Disney's apartment over the firehouse. And that's when I had my fondest memory of Walt Disney.

DP: Can you just describe that?
SB: Sure. We were standing in his apartment. They didn't know what they were going to do with us, so we were all just up there. Of course, it means more to me now than it did back then. But I looked up at him, and he was looking at the gate where the people were walking in, and he had his hands behind his back, and he had a grin from ear to ear. You could see the lump in his throat and the tears coming down his cheeks.

DP: That must have really been a dream come true for him.
SB: Oh, can you imagine that realization for him?

DP: I wanted to ask you about Jimmie Dodd. I know everybody liked him, but I wanted to hear your characterization of him.
SB: Well, you couldn't find a finer human being. He never said anything bad about anybody or anything. He loved and enjoyed life. He didn't preach to you, but he showed you by example what a good human being is. He gave me a little tiny pink jewelry box with a little note that said,

"For your Mousekejewels when you're out on the road." I still have that. It's very special to me. When we were in Australia on our tour, outside the airport, they introduced us to koala bears. And they handed one to him, and its claws dug into him, and there was blood dripping down his arm, and the koala bear relieved itself, it was so scared—or so excited to see a Mouseketeer, Jimmie Dodd! And all the cameras were going, and Jimmie just kept saying, "Isn't he cute? Isn't he darling?"

DP: Karen Pendleton, another Mouseketeer, said that before some of the tours, he would have everybody get together and say a little prayer.
SB: Oh, before all of our shows. And then he had us all over to his house all the time for parties and stuff. And with his wife Ruth Dodd, they were the perfect couple. Roy [Williams] would pretend like he was a big old grouch, but he wasn't. He was like your big uncle.

DP: I was thinking today that some of Jimmie's songs, you know, about proverbs and "Do What the Good Book Says," you couldn't do those on network TV now. That was a real 1950s thing that you could have the religious overtones. It could be on a cable show, but on network TV today? And I think we were all comfortable with it then.
SB: And do you know how many people say to me, "Why don't they have shows like that anymore? That was so much fun."

DP: I think they were great things that he was saying. Not that I always did them, but I thought about them.
SB: And it sounds hokey, but he really lived that. He believed that. That was real. That's the beauty of it. I always think of Jimmie when we do those shows out at Disneyland, that he's not there and we're still doing his songs.

DP: But you probably feel that he's there in spirit.
SB: Oh, definitely he is, of course. He knows that we're carrying that on for him.

DP: I understand that you could type fast and chew gum [at the studio school]. You used to help Bobby Burgess with his math?

SB: Yes, and Annette [Funicello]. We all took Spanish together. Jean Seaman was a wonderful teacher, even though she only had you for three hours a day, and that wasn't consistent. You know, you could rehearse and then come back. You had to do at least twenty minutes [of classroom work] and then go out and shoot, then come back and do twenty more minutes. She was great. By the time I went back to [public] school, I was so far ahead of everyone. Even though they still called me Minnie at school.

DP: Did you have any problems besides being called Minnie?
SB: No, I mean, kids tease kids all the time. You're going to get teased about something. At least it was something that was good and decent, you know.

DP: I noticed in Lorraine Santoli's book, *The Official Mickey Mouse Club Book*, she included a photo of Annette's school notebooks. She had written lots of names, including Zorro, Frankie, and Tab Hunter. I saw Ron Miller's name on there, and I'm guessing that Ron was attractive to all of you. He was a young guy then, too.
SB: Oh, yeah, because he had been a football player, and he would throw the football out on the lawn with the boys. We thought he was very cute. But Annette and I had a terrible crush on Dik Darley. In fact, I had a picture of him under my pillow.

DP: In your spare time, you appeared at Disneyland.
SB: Yeah, it was fun. It's what we wanted to do. And, you know, we used to get there before the park opened, so we would have to warm up the rides. Anyone tell you about that? We used to have contests to see who could spin the cup and saucer the fastest [at the Mad Hatter's Tea Party attraction]. I had to stand up to do it because I was so short. I got calluses on my hands from spinning it. Oh, that was our favorite ride, to do that.

DP: So you never felt sick doing that?
SB: No, the faster you could go, the better it was for me.

DP: Did you warm up the Autopia cars?

SB: Yes, but I wasn't really tall enough for a long time. But yes, we loved that. At home, we had a split rail fence, and our car would pull in, and they'd all come running over and sit on the fence and ask, "What did you do today?"

DP: Did they watch the show?

SB: Yeah. We didn't get to watch the show, because we'd be working when the show was on the air.

DP: I never thought about that.

SB: We saw bits and pieces in the theater when they were editing it.

DP: But you didn't get to see it on a regular basis. I just always assumed that you got to see it.

SB: No, no.

DP: Did you learn how to spell *encyclopedia* like we did from the song?

SB: From Jiminy Cricket. You bet! It's amazing how many people still know that.

DP: It was probably one of the first big words that I knew. You said somewhere that you remember Walt when he came on the set, and he had been painting or something?

SB: Yeah, we were just running around, goofing off, and someone said, "You guys better cool it, there's Walt Disney." "Where, where?" He was in his khakis, and he had paint splashed all over them. He had been in the paint department with the guys. He loved being involved with that. When he'd come on the set, he wouldn't make his presence known. He'd just be very quiet and come in.

DP: Was he friendly?

SB: Oh, yes. He wanted us to call him Uncle Walt. I'm sure you've heard that from many of us. Nobody could because he was Mr. Disney. Uncle Walt didn't seem right. But yeah, we felt he was more of a father figurehead to us all. I told you he wouldn't allow any of the crew to swear around us.

DP: And I guess he didn't smoke around you guys?

SB: No, no. I was shocked when I heard that he had smoked. Bobby ran across him one time, and he was smoking, and Bobby was flabbergasted. But no, he never smoked around us. And, of course, with Annette he was really a father figurehead. She wanted to change her name and he said no, no, no.

DP: When they canceled the show, was the last day a tough one?

SB: Tough, tough day.

DP: How far ahead did you know that it was going off the air?

SB: I don't think too far in advance. Annette and I must have gone through two boxes of Kleenex. And we were doing reaction scenes. We didn't always see who was performing, and they would say, "Okay, now you're watching some good stuff"—you know, just a reaction shot to put in there. We were supposed to be happy and go, "Yay!" And, you know, of course, we're crying, so [director] Sid Miller had a rough time with us. He said, "The more you work, the more we'll all be working together again." And sure enough, way down the road, I'm doing a TV show for Sid and Marty Krofft, and Sidney Miller was doing the voice of one of the characters on the show. So we worked together again. At one point, I had heard that Walt Disney wanted us to grow up and become young adults and just continue the show into adulthood. But that didn't happen.

DP: But I guess in reality only a few of you continued in show business.

SB: Right. Yeah, that's true.

DP: When did you all really get a sense of how popular you were?

SB: Australia. It didn't dawn on us until [the May 1959 and May 1960 tours of] Australia.

DP: The huge crowd at the airport?

SB: Right. There were more people to greet us than greeted Frank Sinatra when he went there. And they broke through the lines. We were coming down those stairs when you deplane, and they broke through the ropes, and they told us get back up the stairs. So we ran back up, and they rolled us through the crowds on the stairs that you board. And then they had bodyguards for each of us. They would pick you up and carry you over the crowds and put you in the car. And after one of our performances, my dad was carrying my costume, and they'd picked me up and put me in the car. My dad was worried about me, and then pretty soon someone grabbed my costume, and it was going down the crowd. My dad was on his knees, and he said, "Oh, my gosh." He was worried about himself. So I'm in the car, and the car is just rocking back and forth, and it's just wall-to-wall faces, and the driver just put it in gear and started driving. It was scary. So that's when I realized.

DP: In some books about the show, they talk about strong competition between the different teams of Mouseketeers. If somebody was shifted to a less favored group, was it humiliating? Did it seem to you at the time like it was strong competition?
SB: When someone was moved to another position, it didn't change my feelings or anything. We were still having fun and [being] kids together. I never saw it as a competition. I just saw it as fun and doing what I wanted to do. What a wonderful life! And you know, I just always looked at it that way. I've never lived for the negative. I guess it's easier when you're short, because it just passes right over your head!

DP: Someone said that being Disney-trained left the Mouseketeers ill equipped to deal with Hollywood realities and ill prepared for the exigencies of a rapidly changing world.
SB: It was great training for me. I had no problem with the changing world out there. The only thing was that maybe you were typecast, because when you would go out for a part, they would say, "Oh, that's Mouseketeer Sharon." That's about the only thing I could consider negative. If anything, it was [also] an icebreaker, and people knew you and it was a good thing.

DP: When you turned twenty-one, you got a special telegram.

SB: Yes, I was working at Litton Data Systems, and Walt Disney sent a telegram.

DP: That's really nice. Just wishing you a happy birthday?
SB: Yeah.

DP: That's great that he would remember.
SB: Yeah.

DP: I remember being at the studio, visiting the archivist, Dave Smith, and he must have taken me through the soundstage where they filmed the twenty-fifth anniversary show, because the original *Mickey Mouse Club* curtains were hanging there. They were in color! I expected them to be black and white. I guess they are still around, because they are in the background when you appeared on the DVD with Leonard Maltin.
SB: They found them packed away. It's amazing enough they weren't in too bad of shape. When we walked in to do that, I had no idea those were going to be hanging there. I walked in, and I just stopped dead in my tracks, and it made my knees buckle. It caught my breath.

DP: On a television show, Mouseketeer Tommy Cole was saying something about how great it was that you were all so comfortable with each other, that the routines just kind of fall into place when you perform now.
SB: We can go several years without seeing each other and sit down and pick right up where we left off before. It's amazing. But yes, when I would go out there and do those [reunion] shows at Disneyland, I'd be doing a number that of course we did when we were kids, and I'd turn and see that same face turning towards me, and it's just a wonderful feeling. And every time, we'll finish a show, like out at Disneyland, and we sing "M-I-C" for the last time, oh, I lump up. It's just like the last day again all over.

DP: Well, that's a really touching song. I haven't been in an audience singing it along with you, but I would think that it would be very emotional for people.
SB: Very touching.

DP: Do you remember what your reaction was to Walt's passing?

SB: Yeah, I was married at the time. We had a nightclub act, Two Cats and a Mouse [Sharon; her husband, Dalton Lee Thomas; and David Jourdan], and we were in Jackpot, Nevada. We had finished a set, and we went to the coffee shop to have a piece of pie. And the drummer came in and said, "Sharon, did you hear Walt Disney died?" I said, "No." And I could tell by the look on my husband's face and the other band members that it was really true. Lee had wanted them to tell me after the evening was over. I ran up to my room and cried. It was just a shock. It came out of left field.

DP: How would you like people to remember Walt Disney?

SB: I've been asked before what is one word to describe Walt Disney, and the only one I can come up with is *Disney*, because he's just one of a kind. He really cared about a good product and entertaining people. He didn't care about the pocketbook, because that was his brother's job. I mean, when you look at things like *Fantasia*, that holds up today. I just think he truly was what he called himself, an Imagineer.

I do wear a lot of Mickey shirts and Disney shirts. I must say, was I brainwashed or what? I just feel warm in them. And I just feel warm and happy inside, that it's something positive and wonderful to people. People say, "Where do I know you from? Where did you go to school? Where did you work?" And it's usually *The Mickey Mouse Club*. Some people will say immediately, "Oh, it's Sharon. It's just a privilege and an honor." "You were in our house every day." "You were our babysitter." "Oh, we learned so much from you, and we always wanted to be like you." It's just so positive and wonderful. Just a glorious feeling.

Index